POSTCARD HISTORY SERIES

Butte

GREETINGS from BUTTE

Metropolis of Montana

© CURT TEICH & CO., INC.

BUTTE, METROPOLIS OF MONTANA. From the census of 1900 through 1940 (about the time this postcard was produced), Butte was the largest city in Montana. Unofficial estimates place Butte's population above 90,000 people in 1917–1918. Both copper prices and the population declined after World War I. Despite the declining population, copper mining remained important, and Butte remains a historically important cosmopolitan Montana city of unique architecture and culture. (Ken Hamlin.)

ON THE FRONT COVER: THE MEN WHO MADE BUTTE. Big capital was necessary to develop the Butte mines, and the "Copper Kings"—William A. Clark, Marcus Daly, and Fritz Augustus Heinze—have received much attention. However, the miners of many ethnicities pictured in this postcard were just as necessary. They toiled in dirty and dangerous jobs with low and sometimes intermittent pay to support their families, and left behind a rich culture still evident in Butte today. (Ken Hamlin.)

ON THE BACK COVER: BUTTE'S BIG ELKS CONVENTION, 1916. Butte is famous for its annual celebrations of the Fourth of July, Miners Union Day, St. Patrick's Day, and others. The large elk statue covered with plaster mixed with high-grade copper ore seen here arching over the intersection of Broadway and Main Streets was created for the state Elks club convention held over the Fourth of July in 1916. The elk statue also symbolizes Butte doing things in a big way. (Ken Hamlin.)

POSTCARD HISTORY SERIES

Butte

Ken Hamlin and Terry and Martha Lonner

ARCADIA
PUBLISHING

Published by Arcadia Publishing
Charleston, South Carolina

Printed in the United States of America

Library of Congress Control Number: 2020949268

For all general information contact Arcadia Publishing at:
Telephone 843-853-2070
Fax 843-853-0044
E-mail sales@arcadiapublishing.com
For customer service and orders:
Toll-Free 1-888-313-2665

Visit us on the Internet at www.arcadiapublishing.com

Dedicated to the people of Butte, Montana: past, present, and future.

CONTENTS

Acknowledgments

We consulted more than 50 books, booklets, and pamphlets previously written about Butte for historical information. In addition, we used newspaper articles from the *Montana Standard*, internet blogs, and videos for historical information. We thank all the authors of these sources for their research and writing.

The Butte–Silver Bow Archives and its staff, including Ellen Crain, Aubry Jaap, and Lindsay Mulcahy, were a great help in resolving some conflicting information. We especially thank Aubry Jaap for reviewing our introductions and captions for historical accuracy. We also thank the following for information: the Montana Bureau of Mines and Geology and Ted Dumaine, the World Museum of Mining and Chance LaDoux, Our Lady of the Rockies Foundation, Main Stope Gallery, Fritz Daily, Lauri Gurnett, Darrell Harding, Connie Kenney, Joe Lee, and Dustin Schillinger.

At times these sources contained conflicting information, and we tried to resolve these issues. All errors that may remain in this book are the responsibility of the authors, not of our consultants.

We thank Tom Mulvaney and David Perlstein for use of postcard images from their collections, and we are pleased to credit them in the captions of their postcards.

Ken Hamlin would like to acknowledge Tom Mulvaney and Jack and Susan Davis for inspiring his interest in collecting postcards and other Montana ephemera. Ken also gratefully thanks his wife, Pat, for her encouragement in writing and for putting up with his collecting obsession and scattering "musty old stuff" around the house.

Terry and Martha Lonner thank their Butte family members and friends for providing them with many fond memories of growing up in the "Richest Hill on Earth," and as they say, "You can take the kid out of Butte, but you can't take Butte out of the kid." Two of Terry's relatives died in the Butte mines.

We thank the staff of Arcadia Publishing for all their cheerful direction and assistance, without which this book would have been difficult to publish.

All images not otherwise credited are from the collection of Ken Hamlin.

INTRODUCTION

The wicked, wealthy, hospitable, full-blooded little city [of Butte] welcomed me with wild enthusiasm of the most disorderly kind.

—Theodore Roosevelt, 1903

In the late spring of 1864, miners found placer gold along what became Silver Bow Creek and its surrounding gulches. By summer, a mining district had formed, and many camps occupied the valley from Silver Bow junction to what became Butte. Enough miners were in the area for the government to authorize a post office called Butte City on July 20, 1868.

The gold was low grade, containing many impurities, and brought only about half the price paid at Virginia City and other mining areas. Placer gold was soon depleted, and by 1870, many miners had left the district. A few stayed to explore the quartz lodes, and found some relatively rich silver deposits. One of the first was the Astroid claim (later to become the Travona), found by William Farlin in 1864. Other claims were filed, but the silver ore required large capital input for the milling and smelting that would make mining cost-effective, so the population remained low.

William A. Clark, who had acquired wealth through businesses at Virginia City, Helena, and Deer Lodge, came to Butte and acquired several mining properties. He and others constructed some improved mills and small smelters. By the mid-1870s, it became apparent that silver mining, not gold, was the future for Butte City. After assaying some ore from Butte City, the Walker brothers of Salt Lake City, Utah, sent mining engineer Marcus Daly to Butte City in 1876 to investigate the silver lodes. Daly found numerous lodes to be rich and began purchasing them. The first successful local milling and smelting of silver ore also occurred in 1876, silver became important in Butte's economy, and the population increased.

Marcus Daly is usually credited with finding the first large copper vein and understanding its importance. However, Clark had also investigated the value of the large copper deposits, and opened the Colorado & Montana Smelter in 1879. Thomas Edison patented the electric light bulb in 1880, and the use of copper for lights and power transmission began. Nikola Tesla's invention of the alternating-current induction motor in 1888 led to the invention and production of household appliances in the early 1900s and was of major importance to mining and the price of copper. Silver sustained Butte as a large Montana mining city through the 1880s, but copper mining made it the metropolis it was after that, likely reaching its peak population in 1917–1918.

Many immigrants came to Butte to work in the silver mines in the 1880s. More came with the expanding copper mining industry after 1880 and its boom in the early 1900s as demand for copper increased. The fame of Butte as an employer reached worldwide, as evidenced by this quote from Mary Hagan (etched on the wall of the Butte–Silver Bow Archives) as her daughter and husband prepared to leave by ship from England (via Ireland) to Butte to find work: "Now don't forget, Lizzie, when you get to the new world, don't stop in America. You go straight to Butte, Montana."

Butte and copper mining were inseparable from the late 1880s through two world wars to the 1970s. Copper and other minerals mined in Butte supplied much of the nation's necessary metal for war production and armaments and for the increased standard of living resulting from electrification and labor-saving appliances. By the 1950s, ore from the underground mines was of increasingly lower quality, and mining was less profitable. The Anaconda Copper Mining Company (ACM) began its famous Berkeley Pit open-pit mine in July 1955 as a more cost-effective way to mine low-grade ores. Some underground mining continued for a while, but significant ore production by underground mining ended about 1975. The Atlantic Richfield Company did some exploratory underground mining but halted that in 1979. The New Butte Mining Company purchased some underground mines in 1987 and did exploratory mining but ended its underground operations in 1993. The Berkeley Pit ceased operations in 1982, the water pumps in the Kelley mine were turned off, and "the Pit" began filling with toxic contaminated water; it is now a large Superfund site.

The three Copper Kings of Butte, Clark, Daly, and Heinze, have received much attention, but the immigrant miners, small business owners of all kinds, laborers, saloon keepers, "soiled doves," and others gave Butte its character, personality, and grit. Immigrants from more than 30 ethnicities provided a diversity and rich culture that is still characteristic of Butte's reduced population of about 35,000 today.

The use of postcards as the early-20th-century equivalent of today's email began in about 1903 and reached its peak during 1907–1915, the "Golden Age" of postcards, when millions were produced and mailed. During the early 1900s, Kodak began producing a camera with which real-photo picture postcards of people, events, activities, and scenery could be printed on special card stock, millions of which were sent to friends and relatives.

The postcard craze of the 1910s coincided with the peak of Butte's population, and as the largest city in Montana, likely more postcards in quantity and type were produced for Butte than any other Montana town.

Most pre-1905 postcards of Butte were printed by the Detroit Photographic Company (Detroit Publishing Company after 1905). After 1907, many other national publishers began printing postcards of Butte. As one might expect, as a large town and large market, Butte began to see local businesses become postcard publishers and printers. Butte publishers and printers included Keefe Brothers Post Office News Stand (or Store), Julius Fried, Cohn Brothers, McKee Printing, Northwest Postcard and Souvenir Company, the Postcard Shop, B.E. Calkins, Bessette-Stork Company, Bessette-Casey Company, Jennings and Gunsdorf, Silver Bow News Company, Cecil Nixon, and Allied Printing. Lauretta Studio (Archie and Lauretta Walkup) produced many 1950s–1970s chrome-type postcards of Butte.

Some of the scenes on the postcards that follow appear in other books about Butte. However, many readers are unlikely to have previously seen other of our postcard views and scenes. Additionally, the messages on many postcards provide interesting and unique explanations of the views or social history context. We hope you enjoy the images on these postcards, possibly learn a little more about Butte history, and appreciate the diversity, character, and multiethnic culture of the men who toiled in the mines, those who made their living supporting miners, and the women and children who also worked, gave support, and made up the families of Butte.

One

MINING AND LABOR

Mining was why Butte became known as the "Metropolis of Montana" and the "Richest Hill on Earth." From 1880 to 2000, the Butte hill produced almost 50 percent of the nation's and 25 percent of the world's copper and significant quantities of other minerals. This production amounted to 22,799,000,000 pounds of copper (11,399,500 tons), 3,702,787,341 pounds of manganese, 854,797,405 pounds of lead, 326,671,890 pounds of molybdenum (used in steel production), 725,486,448 ounces of silver, and 2,922,446 ounces of gold from about 500 mines operating over the course of Butte's history. Several mines had vertical shafts between 3,000 and 5,300 feet deep, with all mines totalling 10,000 miles of underground workings.

Immigrants from around the world came to Butte to make a better living, and most were hard working and dedicated to providing for families anxiously waiting for them to come home after their dangerous shift was done. They were proud of their work, camaraderie, ingenuity, and expertise in making and using equipment to create new methods to get the rock to the surface in a safe and efficient manner. The mineral production by Butte miners contributed substantially to improving the standard of living in America and winning two world wars.

Mining is arduous, dirty, and dangerous, and Butte historian James Harrington estimated over 2,200 Butte miners directly lost their lives while working. Additionally, many (an estimated 42 percent in a 1916–1919 study) suffered debilitating injury accidents and illnesses, such as "miner's consumption" (silicosis), that made them miserable and reduced their lifespan. The economics of mining the increasingly lower-quality ore led to open-pit mining in 1955 (Berkeley Pit).

The combination of unsafe working conditions and conflicts over wages resulted in labor disputes, strikes, and sometimes violence. The first labor strike in Butte was in 1878, leading to the formation of the Butte Workingmen's Union. It reorganized in 1885 as the Butte Miner's Union. In 1893, the Butte Miner's Union took the lead and became Local No. 1 of the broader Western Federation of Miners. Almost all other crafts (at least 34) in Butte, including newsboys, formed unions, and Butte became known as the "Gibraltar of Unionism."

COPPER MINE, BUTTE, MONT.

EARLY COPPER MINING. This postcard shows a view of early mining in Butte when lighting was by candles and ore was moved by wheelbarrow. Drilling holes for placement of dynamite was done by hand, with one man hitting the drill head with a hammer and the other turning the drill after each stroke. Hand-drilling was featured in mining contests on Miner's Union Day in Butte long after it was abandoned in the mines.

BUTTE MINERS GOING ON SHIFT, BUTTE, MONT.

MINERS GOING ON SHIFT. This early view of Butte miners going on shift shows them with three candles in their coat pockets (white patches), lunch buckets (for some, a traditional pasty), and no hard hats. Before carbide lanterns or electrification, three candles provided lighting for an eight-hour shift. The 1907 writing reads: "over 15,000 men work under the ground, mostly foreigners."

10

MINING IN MONTANA. DRILLING.

MECHANICAL AND AIR-POWERED DRILLING. Large-scale mines used mechanical and air-powered drills as soon as they became available. This method of drilling was especially necessary for lower-grade ore and for the very deep mines in Butte. Note the lack of hard hats and primitive bracing in this pre-1906 postcard view.

Miners at Lunch, 2,000 Feet Underground, Butte, Mont.

NO. 19

LUNCH AT 2,000 FEET UNDERGROUND. These miners and their lunch buckets are 2,000 feet underground. The miner on the right appears to be holding a Cornish pasty, a pastry filled with beef, diced potatoes, and onions folded into a half circle and baked. Some also included rutabaga or carrots. Many Butte miners were from Cornwall, England, and the pasty remains a favorite meal in Butte today.

ANACONDA MINE

ST. LAWRENCE MINE.—SOME BUTTE, MONTANA, MINES.

NO. 1061   W. G. MACFARLANE, PUBLISHER, TORONTO, CANADA.

ANACONDA AND ST. LAWRENCE MINES. One of the earliest postcards of Butte, published between 1901 and 1903, pictures the iconic Anaconda mine and the adjacent St. Lawrence mine. Originally a silver mine discovered by Michael Hickey, the Anaconda was purchased by Marcus Daly and developed as a copper producer. With the acquisition of many nearby mines such as the St. Lawrence, he established the Anaconda Copper Mining Company and his fortune.

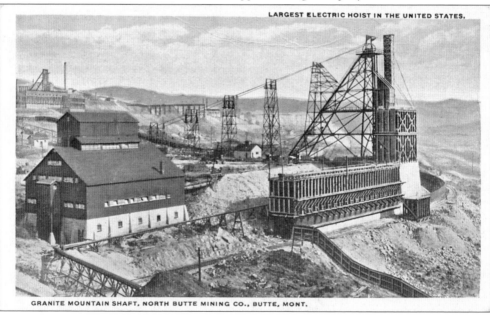

LARGEST ELECTRIC HOIST IN THE UNITED STATES.

GRANITE MOUNTAIN SHAFT, NORTH BUTTE MINING CO., BUTTE, MONT.

GRANITE MOUNTAIN MINE. On June 8, 1917, a fire broke out in the Granite Mountain mine, pictured here after the fire. A carbide lamp ignited an oil-soaked electrical cable that was being installed, and smoke spread to the adjacent Speculator mine shaft. In the greatest metals mine disaster in US history, 168 miners died, mostly from asphyxiation due to smoke inhalation. About 250 miners survived.

THE SPECULATOR MINE. Smoke from the Granite Mountain mine fire filled the adjacent and connected Speculator mine, limiting escape routes for miners in both mines. Miners Manus Duggan and J.D. Moore, who both perished, were credited as heroes for saving other miners. Moore left a note reading, "You will know your Jim died like a man and his last thought was for the wife that I love better than anyone on earth. Tell mother and the boys goodbye."

THE PENNSYLVANIA MINE. On Valentine's Day 1916, a fire at the Pennsylvania mine killed 21 men, the second deadliest single-day mine disaster in Butte. The Pennsylvania had been owned by a number of people and companies but at the time of the fire was owned by the ACM. The location of the Pennsylvania mine is now within the Berkeley Pit.

SMELTER SCENE, TAPPING THE BLAST FURNACE. SEEING BUTTE CAR, BUTTE, MONT.

SMELTERS IN BUTTE. Small, inefficient smelters for silver ore were constructed in Butte as early as 1868, but more efficient smelters were constructed during 1875–1881. The first successful smelter for copper ore in Butte was built about 1879, and W.A. Clark, F.A. Heinze, and others built numerous smelters in Butte after that. Marcus Daly built a large smelter in 1883 to process his copper ore and also built the town of Anaconda nearby.

CLARK'S REDUCTION WORKS SMOKESTACK. W.A. Clark purchased the Butte Reduction Works in 1887. In the 1890s, the *Anaconda Standard* newspaper, Butte mayor Henry Mueller, and others castigated the Butte Reduction Works for its smoke pollution. The 353-foot stack (the tallest in the world at that time) was Clark's attempt in 1906 to reduce local pollution. In 1918, the ACM outdid Clark by building the 585-foot stack at Anaconda, the largest still-standing masonry stack in the world.

14

BUTTE HOIST COMPRESSOR PLANT.
After the days of hand-drilling, mining companies produced compressed air to operate hoists and drilling equipment. The ACM produced compressed air at three locations: the Leonard, the Bell, and the High Ore. This real-photo postcard likely shows the largest plant at the High Ore, which by 1922 supplied compressed air for 22 ACM mines.

HOIST AT LEONARD MINE.
The Leonard mine was often used as the "show" mine, where dignitaries and local groups could see underground workings. In 1912, the new compressed-air plant at the Leonard mine was touted as the most extensive in the world. Hoists at the Mountain View, High Ore, and Diamond mines were operated by this plant. Many mines later converted to electricity for hoisting.

MOUNTAIN CON(SOLIDATED) MINE. The Mountain Con mine was near the top of the Butte Hill east of Main Street, near Centerville. The headframe still stands. Operating until 1974, the Mountain Con was one of the last active underground mines. In 1961, the main shaft reached over 5,300 feet deep, giving authenticity to the phrase "Butte, a mile high and a mile deep."

THE ORIGINAL MINE. W.A. Clark patented the Original mine in 1878, but the steel gallows frame shown in this postcard was not erected until 1898. The ACM acquired the mine in 1910, and it operated into the 1970s. The mine encompassed two blocks between Main, Montana, Woolman, and Copper Streets. The headframe was preserved and can be viewed today at 443 North Main Street.

THE GAGNON MINE. The Gagnon mine was another W.A. Clark–owned property adjacent to the Original mine in the Centerville district. Both were surrounded by residential and business properties. It was acquired by the ACM in 1910 along with other Clark properties. The Gagnon was one of the last operating underground mines.

THE RARUS MINE. F.A. Heinze purchased the Rarus mine in 1895 and found some rich ore bodies, and the Rarus became a major copper producer. The Rarus featured in many court battles, as Heinze also accessed ore from the mining properties of others through the Rarus shaft. Heinze sold all of his properties to Amalgamated Copper Company in 1906 and left Montana. The site of the Rarus mine is now within the Berkeley Pit.

THE CORA MINE. The Cora was a mining property in the Centerville district operated by F.A. Heinze. On May 12, 1905, seven miners were killed and one injured in a dynamite explosion at the 1,500-foot level. Reports at the time speculated that hot wax from a candle carried by a foreman who was bundling up dynamite packages caused the explosion.

ANACONDA AND NEVERSWEAT MINES. The Anaconda (left) and Neversweat mines (right with its iconic seven stacks) are among the famed mines swallowed by the Berkeley Pit. The International Workers of the World called a strike on April 19, 1920. On April 21, picketing miners gathered at the Neversweat mine, and ACM guards opened fire, hitting 16 miners and killing one. Federal troops arrived on April 22 to quell the disturbance.

MOONLIGHT MINE, 1903. The Moonlight mine was south of the Neversweat mine at the east end of Granite Street. In this postcard view, Finn Town, a bastion of Finnish miners, is just to the right and extends behind the viewer. The Moonlight was another mine swallowed by the Berkeley Pit.

MOUNTAIN VIEW MINE. The Mountain View mine was east of the Anaconda and Neversweat mines, and it too became part of the Berkeley Pit. Originally, the Mountain View mine was part of the Lewisohn brothers' Boston & Montana Company (B&M), but Amalgamated Copper Company acquired majority ownership of B&M in 1901. The railroad cars at center are unloading timbers for shoring up the mine shafts, drifts, and stopes.

HIGH ORE MINE. The High Ore mine, so named because of its original high-grade ore, was in the eastern (Meaderville) mining district. It became part of the ACM properties and eventually part of the Berkeley Pit. The writer of this postcard sent to a girlfriend in Great Falls, Montana, says that he had a fine time at Columbia Gardens that evening, July 7, 1910.

MINNIE HEALY MINE. The rich Minnie Healy mine, located between Meaderville and McQueen and owned by F. Augustus Heinze, featured in the court battles between Heinze and the Amalgamated Copper Company (later Anaconda) in 1904. Heinze sold all his Butte mining properties to Amalgamated (controlled by Standard Oil) in 1906 for $10.5 million, but Amalgamated manipulated Heinze's United Copper Company stock and ruined him.

Pittsmont Mine, Butte, Mont.

PITTSMONT MINE(S). The four Pittsmont mines were on the east side of the Butte mining district, between McQueen and Columbia Gardens. Operated from 1902 to 1930 by the East Butte Copper Mining Company, this company had the only smelter in the 1920s not owned by the ACM. The Pittsmont mines are near or within the area of the Continental Pit, operated since the 1980s by Montana Resources and producing copper and, importantly, molybdenum for steel production.

BUTTE'S FIRST ZINC MILL, BUTTE AND SUPERIOR MINING CO., BUTTE, MONT.

BUTTE'S FIRST ZINC MILL. The Butte & Superior Mining Company owned the Germania mine. Originally a silver producer, common at the outer edges of the Butte mining district, the Germania began producing mostly zinc and manganese during World War I. After construction of the zinc mill pictured here, the Germania mine was one of Montana's largest producers of zinc. The Lexington mine also produced considerable zinc ore.

Unloading Timbers at Stewart Mine, Butte, Montana

Mule Train 1100 ft. level, "Rarus Mine", BUTTE, Mont.

TIMBER FOR BUTTE MINES. As seen in this postcard of the Stewart (properly Steward) mine, massive amounts of timber were necessary for bracing the mine shafts and as fuel. As local areas such as the Highland and Pintler mountain ranges and others were mostly depleted of timber, the ACM expanded its logging business to the Missoula area, including near Bonner and in the Bitterroot Valley.

MULES IN THE MINES. Mules were used to pull ore cars underground within the mines through about 1915, when more electrification occurred. This postcard, made from an N.A. Forsyth photograph, shows one of the mule ore cars 1,100 feet underground in the Rarus mine. Once the mules were underground, most never saw the light of day again. A few lucky ones were retired and hoisted back above ground.

ELECTRIC MOTOR LOCOMOTIVES REPLACE MULES. After 1914, electricity gradually replaced methods of hoisting, lighting, and ventilation in the mines. By 1923, the ACM had retired all but two mules transporting ore carts underground in the mines and replaced them with 200 four-ton electric locomotives for hauling ore from mining faces to the hoists.

MONTANA POWER COMPANY ELECTRIC SUBSTATION. This 1920s postcard shows the Montana Power Company's (MPC) electric substation with the High Ore mine gallows frame at left and the Mountain View mine gallows frame at top center. John Ryan started the MPC in 1912 by acquiring and consolidating smaller electric companies to sell power to the ACM and the Milwaukee Railroad. With continued acquisitions and building, the MPC ended up supplying electric power to most of western Montana.

BERKELEY PIT LOOKING NORTH, 1960s. Open-pit mining started replacing underground mining in Butte with the opening of the Berkeley Pit in 1955. By the time the Pit ceased operation in 1982, it was more than a mile long and wide, and the depth from the rim to the bottom was about 1,800 feet. An estimated 1 billion tons of material were removed during its operation.

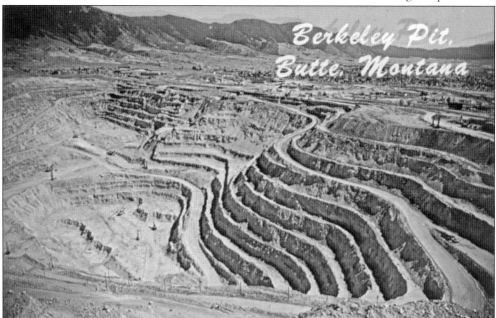

BERKELEY PIT LOOKING SOUTHEAST, 1960s. The Pit forever changed the landscape of Butte, engulfing many underground mines and the communities of Meaderville, McQueen, East Butte, and Finn Town. After mining underground ceased, the water pumps were turned off in the Kelley mine, and the Pit began filling with toxic acidic water and dissolved metals to the depth of about 1,100 feet in 2020. It is now a Superfund site.

THE CLYDE E. WEED CONCENTRATOR. The Clyde E. Weed concentrator was built in 1963–1964 to process lower-quality ores from the Berkeley and later Continental Pits. Weed, a mining engineer, advanced to become president of the ACM in 1956 and chairman and chief executive officer in 1964. He retired in 1965.

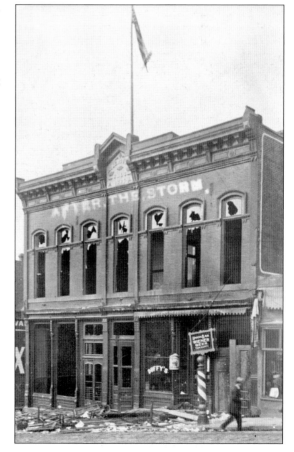

BUTTE MINER'S UNION HALL. On Miner's Union Day, June 13, 1914, miners upset with representation by the Western Federation of Miners (WFM) attacked union and city officials in the parade. On June 21, a newly formed rebel union of about 2,000 members under Muckie McDonald attacked the Miner's Union Hall, destroying the interior. They carried away the safe and threw acting mayor Frank Curran out the second-floor window, breaking his arm and dislocating his ankle. (Courtesy of Tom Mulvaney.)

MINER'S UNION HALL DYNAMITED.
On June 23, 1914, the rebel union prepared to dynamite the hall with about 200 WFM members inside. The members escaped through a fire escape in back just before the building was blown up. The sender of this postcard was present and assured his mother and father that he was safe. Because of these union representation struggles, Butte, the former union stronghold, became an open shop controlled by mining companies from 1914 to 1934.

FRANK LITTLE. Representing the Industrial Workers of the World, Frank Little arrived in Butte on July 18, 1917, to help lead a strike against the ACM. Early on August 1, six masked men broke into the boardinghouse where he was staying. He was beaten, abducted, dragged behind a car, and hanged from a railroad trestle. No one was arrested or prosecuted for his death. An estimated 13,500 people attended his funeral procession in Butte.

Two

COLUMBIA GARDENS AND RECREATION

In 1888, John Gordan and Fredrick Ritchie, owners of the Variety Theater, leased the Adams Columbia property east of Butte and built a picnic grounds, dance hall, restaurant, playground, and zoo. Good transportation to the area was lacking, and the endeavor was not successful. In 1899, Copper King W.A. Clark decided to construct a family amusement park for Butte and bought the property from Adams. He appointed Jesse Wharton, the manager of his Butte Electric Railway system, to also manage his proposed family amusement park. After tearing down old buildings and constructing new ones, the park opened in June 1899 with no admission fee and transportation provided by newly constructed tracks of the Butte Electric Railway. By 1906, Columbia Gardens was the major recreational attraction for Butte and the surrounding area. Attractions included a pavilion and dance hall, grandstand and sports field, theater, roller coaster, Ferris wheel, merry-go-round, herbarium, fish hatchery, zoo, picnic grove, tennis courts, playground, miniature railroad, arcade, cafe, ice cream parlor, popcorn, and more. During the summer, Thursday was Children's Day, which included free transportation on the Butte Electric Railway for all Silver Bow County children. Butte's championship high school football teams of 1907 and 1908 played their games at Columbia Gardens.

Over the years 1899–1925, Clark invested millions of dollars in the 68-acre facility, and it is estimated that his Butte Electric Railway had an annual $50,000 operating loss due to reduced fares to Columbia Gardens. On Clark's final visit to Butte, he stated that no investment during his lifetime had paid better dividends than Columbia Gardens. Clark died in 1925, and his estate sold Columbia Gardens and other properties to the Anaconda Company in 1928. Services and features were gradually cut back until the ACM closed Columbia Gardens in 1973. Shortly thereafter, fire destroyed much of Columbia Gardens. Similar to Clark, the ACM lost money on Columbia Gardens every year except 1929.

Also presented in this chapter are postcards of some other recreational pursuits of Butte citizens, such as sports, music, hunting, fishing, and parades, but for generations, Columbia Gardens was Butte's crown jewel of recreation.

BALLOON ASCENSION AT COLUMBIA GARDENS. This photograph was taken by N.A. Forsyth, who came to Butte in 1902 and had a studio here from 1904 to 1930 producing stereo views. This 1906–1907 view (roller coaster constructed in 1906), also produced as a stereo view, shows the first pavilion (at center) in the Columbia Gardens, constructed in 1900 and burned in October 1907.

SECOND PAVILION AT COLUMBIA GARDENS. After the first pavilion burned in October 1907, a new pavilion, seen in this postcard, was constructed and completed on May 7, 1909. A celebratory grand ball was held in the new dance palace with about 3,000 people in attendance. Some of Columbia Gardens' famous flower displays can be seen in the foreground, and the boating lake is in the left background.

The Grand Stand at The Gardens, Butte, Mont.

THE GRANDSTAND AT THE GARDENS. Butte has always been famous for its love of sports, so Clark ordered construction of a sports complex at Columbia Gardens in 1902. It included a grandstand and bleachers that could hold up to 3,000 people. Until Clark Park in Butte was completed in 1921, the grandstand complex was the main athletic facility for baseball, football, soccer, rugby, boxing, horse races, and the annual June 13 Miner's Union Day competitions.

Herbarium and Fish Hatchery, Butte, Mont., at Columbia Gardens.

HERBARIUM AND FISH HATCHERY. Another major complex at Columbia Gardens was the herbarium and fish hatchery. The herbarium's major function was to supply flowers for the gardens' famous floral displays and also the trees seen in the foreground to form shady groves. The Butte Angler's Club, formed in 1903 in cooperation with Clark, raised fish from eggs at the hatchery to stock the Big Hole River, Butte's favorite fishing stream.

A View in Columbia Gardens, Butte, Mont.

THE GARDENS' FLORAL DISPLAYS. This postcard view presents one of the gardens' famous and popular floral displays. The ringed walkways are flanked by the popular butterfly and crossed American flag displays. Anchors, stars, and the insignia of the Butte Miner's Union were also popular. The very first floral display in 1901 spelled out "Columbia Gardens." A crew of more than 30 workers was required to run the greenhouse and maintain the displays.

A View in Columbia Gardens, Butte, Mont. 58.

THE LYRE FLORAL DISPLAY. The popular lyre display was appropriate because of the many musical events at Columbia Gardens. The famous Boston & Montana Band performed here, along with nationally famous bands such as Glenn Miller, Duke Ellington, Benny Goodman, Guy Lombardo, Frank Yankovic (polkas were very popular), Harry James, and Tommy Dorsey. Dances and high school proms were held here until the gardens closed in 1973.

COLUMBIA GARDENS, 1920S VIEW. This real-photo postcard shows a broad view of Columbia Gardens in the 1920s, after the planted trees had grown substantially. The wooden roller coaster installed in 1906 traverses the center, and the Ferris wheel installed just after that is at left, behind the roller coaster. They were the only amusement rides of their kind in Montana. The grandstand sports complex is at top center.

ROLLER COASTER, FERRIS WHEEL, AND CAROUSEL. All three of the most popular rides at Columbia Gardens are shown in this 1920s real-photo postcard. The Ferris wheel and carousel merry-go-round entrances were close to each other, and one end of the roller coaster is behind, with cowboy swings in the playground to the right. The pavilion is to the left, just out of view.

COLUMBIA GARDENS PANORAMA, 1906. This trifold postcard shows a panoramic view of Columbia Gardens looking southeast about 1906, just before a fire destroyed the first pavilion (center, near right fold). The fish hatchery and herbarium are in the background of the middle

COLUMBIA

COLUMBIA GARDENS PANORAMA, 1930s. This 1930s panorama view of Columbia Gardens approximately matches the center and right panels of the view above. The new pavilion is at left. The low arcade building, constructed in 1910, is in the middle panel, with the roller coaster to

a Gardens, Butte, Mont.

panel (note the newly planted trees between the herbarium and pavilion). The grandstand sports complex is under the right fold. The man-made lake is at far right. (Courtesy of Tom Mulvaney.)

E. MONTANA

the right. To the right of the roller coaster is the tower for the new biplane ride. The lake area was drained and converted to parking and a picnic area by the 1930s.

BUTTE HIGH SCHOOL FOOTBALL TEAM, '07
Champions of the Northwest

NORTHWEST FOOTBALL CHAMPIONS, 1907. The Butte High School football team were the champions of Montana for 13 of 16 years between 1900 and 1916. The team defeated Billings 27-0 for the championship in 1907. On November 16, they defeated the Spokane, Washington, team in Butte by a score of 5-4 (scoring was different in those days) in front of 6,000 people for the unofficial championship of the Northwest.

SPOKANE PROTESTS THE WIN. In December, Spokane lodged a protest of Butte's win, stating that Butte's Reno Schroeder (second from left) had completed high school in Wisconsin earlier that year, and that teammate Joseph Phillips was over 21 years of age. Spokane requested that all of Butte's Montana wins be forfeit. The Montana State Interscholastic Association did not sustain the protest.

QUESTIONS REMAIN. Joseph Phillips is at far right in this photograph of the 1907 team. Butte principal George Downer was said to have been the principal at the Wisconsin school the year Schroeder graduated, and Phillips was from there as well. Butte beat Miles City 40-0 for the Montana championship in 1908, won the western championship, and then lost to Chicago in Butte 11-4 for the unofficial national title.

BUTTE'S FOURTH OF JULY, 1908. "Biggest Doin's in the History of Montana," reads the firecracker. Butte is well known for its celebrations and parades. This postcard advertisement by McKee Printing is uncommon, but McKee produced similar comic advertisements on business envelopes through the 1920s. Events advertised included fireworks, boxing, baseball, parades, bands, carnivals, and circuses. Butte did have the largest celebrations in Montana from the 1900s to 1920s.

ELKS CONVENTION, JULY 4, 1916. The Elks Lodge paid local stage designer Edmund Carns $4,000 to build an elk arch for the parade. The elk was 62 feet tall, 44 feet long, and covered with plaster mixed with high-grade copper ore, giving it a greenish patina. The photographer is looking east on Broadway Street, and the elk is facing south on Main Street. The Hirbour Tower is to the left.

ELK ARCH LOOKING WEST. This view shows the photographer looking west on Broadway Street. The First National Bank is to the rear of the elk. The two real-photo postcards of the elk arch in combination indicate the transition in progress during 1916 between horse-drawn delivery wagons (this card) and the newer automobiles (previous view). The street railway cars also could pass under the elk.

ELKS MEMBERS ON PARADE. This third real-photo postcard view shows Elks members parading south down Main Street on July 4, 1916. The elk arch at left is at the intersection of Main and Broadway Streets. An estimated 3,000 Elks from across Montana attended the 1916 convention in Butte. Identifiable buildings on the right (east) include Ley's Jewelers, Red Boot Shoe Company, the Hirbour Tower, and Hennessy's. (Courtesy of Tom Mulvaney.)

ELEPHANTS ON MONTANA STREET, 1909. Amateur photographer W.J. Boast took this real-photo postcard of the Ringling Brothers circus parade on August 6, 1909. The elephants are headed south on Montana Street. The First Baptist Church, built two years earlier, is at far right on the corner of West Broadway Street. Mayer Electric Company, an assay office, and Butte Coal Company are also visible on the west side of Montana Street. (Courtesy of Tom Mulvaney.)

INDIANS CAMPED NEAR TIMBER BUTTE. This 1908 real-photo postcard shows a partial view of some of the landless Cree, Chippewa, and Metis Indians who camped near the Butte city dump. They lived off dump refuse in summer and county welfare in winter. As payback for help, they usually staged two-day celebrations for the people of Butte that included horse races, war dances, and roasted horses, dogs, ground squirrels, and rats. (Courtesy of Tom Mulvaney.)

BUTTE FISHERMEN. Fishing was so popular in Butte that in the May 22, 1901, *Butte Inter Mountain* newspaper, the Oregon Short Line Railway advertised "Fisherman's Rates—To Divide—$1.00, Melrose—$1.50, Glen—$2.00 (all Big Hole river). On Saturdays and Sundays, good to return the following Monday." The Kodak 3A camera leaning against the creel was produced from 1903 through 1915 primarily to produce real-photo postcards like this one of Meaderville fishermen.

Red Rock Lake, Butte's Hunting Resort.

BUTTE HUNTERS. The Butte Rod & Gun Club organized in 1880. Hunting opportunities, especially for the common man, soon diminished near Butte. In the early 1900s, some of Butte's wealthier hunters within the club established a duck and goose hunting resort at Red Rocks Lake in the Centennial Valley south of Dillon. Their land became federal property when Red Rocks Wildlife Refuge was established in 1935.

FIRST AIRPLANE IN BUTTE. Eugene Ely flew the first airplane into Butte at the fairgrounds on June 9, 1911. He also flew exhibitions at four other Montana cities. Fellow aviation pioneer Cromwell Dixon was the first to fly over the Continental Divide near Helena on September 30. Dixon died on October 2, 1911, in a crash at Spokane, Washington, and Eugene Ely died on October 18, 1911, when he crashed at the Georgia State Fair at Macon.

FAMOUS BOSTON & MONTANA BAND. The Boston & Montana Mining Company asked Cornishman Sam Treloar to organize a company band in 1887. It became the ACM Band when the Boston & Montana Company was acquired by the Anaconda Company, and the Butte Mines Band after 1919. The band performed nationally and won three national competitions. Frank Burke, the short drum major in the white uniform at front, became a mascot for the Cincinnati Reds baseball team.

BUTTE'S BEEF TRAIL. This 2003 postcard promoted a video documentary about a pioneering ski area five miles southwest of Butte. The Butte Ski Club formed an all-volunteer nonprofit organization in 1937. It bought and developed the Beef Trail Ski Area, and 3,000 people attended its grand opening in 1939. It served people of all ages, incomes, and abilities for 50 years. Some skiers who trained there became local and state champions, with a few attaining national acclaim.

Three

PERSONALITIES

Although "personalities" can be interpreted as famous or important people, it can also be read as "unusual characters." The town of Butte itself, with its wide ethnic diversity and history, has its own personality or character. "No Smoking" was printed in 14 languages on a sign in the mines. The ethnic diversity of miners and the service industry included Irish, Cornish, Jewish, Chinese, Serbians, Croatians, Slovenians, Montenegrins, Danish, Welsh, Greeks, Scandinavians, Mexicans, African Americans, Lebanese/Syrians, Finnish, Italians, French, and Germans. It is no wonder that this mix produced many personalities. Butte remains full of interesting individual personalities and characters today.

The postcards in this chapter emphasize only the few Butte–Silver Bow personalities who appear on or have a connection with a postcard. Butte historians will remember many others not represented here, including "Fat Jack" (John Codman Jones), a hack driver who carried many celebrities including presidents, movie stars, business tycoons, and others from the depot to their hotel. A more recent example is "Tony the Trader" (Anthony A. Canonica), who was famous for his antique (junk) shop and a regular participant in Butte's Fourth of July parades, including being grand marshal in 1981.

The list could be almost endless, but a few important personalities who were born and raised in Butte and Silver Bow County include football legends Milt Popovich, Bob O'Billovich, Sonny Holland, Sonny Lubick, and Jim Sweeney. Others include longtime sheriff Bob Butorovich, motorcycle daredevil and entertainer Robert (Evel) Knievel, potter Rudy Autio, politician Arnold Olsen, and novelists Myron Brining and Donald McCaig.

Montana's first and to date only female governor, Judy Martz, was born in Big Timber but lived in Butte after age five. She was also an Olympic speed skater and Miss Rodeo Montana in 1962. Mary MacLane and her shocking (for the time, 1902–1917) autobiographical books brought attention to Butte. There are many other more recent personalities associated with Butte, including some not born here, who could be mentioned, but turn the page to see Butte personalities with a connection to postcards.

Marcus Daly Memorial, Butte, Mont.

COPPER KING MARCUS DALY.
Marcus Daly invested in Butte silver mines in 1876 and found the first large copper vein. Later, he built a smelter, the town of Anaconda, the Butte, Anaconda & Pacific Railroad, and the town of Hamilton. The statue of Daly by famed sculptor Augustus Saint-Gaudens was unveiled on September 2, 1907, in the center of Main Street near the Federal Building. It was moved to the Montana School of Mines in June 1941.

WILLIAM ANDREWS CLARK MANSION, BUTTE. One of Butte's Copper Kings, W.A. Clark's 27-room mansion at 219 West Granite Street was started in 1884 and finished in 1888. In his lifetime, Senator Robert La Follette called Clark "one of the 100 men who owned America." One estimate of the value of his estate when he died in 1925 was over four billion in today's dollars, making him one of the wealthiest Americans ever. Tours of his mansion are offered today.

CLARK'S FOLLY, NEW YORK CITY. Clark had a larger, 121-room mansion built on Fifth Avenue in New York City. It was completed in 1911 and demolished in 1927. Clark died in 1925 at the age of 86 in this mansion. Contemporary reviews were generally negative, but some later architectural critics said that it would have been considered great if an establishment figure had owned it.

FRITZ AUGUSTUS HEINZE. Heinze came to Butte in 1889 as a mining engineer for the Boston & Montana Company after Clark and Daly were well established. His modern smelters, seen in this postcard, could offer lower-cost smelting to small companies. His Rarus mine was a premier property, and by 1902, he was considered one of Butte's three Copper Kings. After many court battles, he sold his properties to the Amalgamated in 1906.

General View of Heinze Smelters, Montana.

KATHLYN WILLIAMS. Few remember silent film star and native daughter Kathlyn Williams, born Kathleen Mabel Williams in Butte on May 31, 1879. Copper King William Clark paid for her training at the Sargent School of Acting in New York City. She appeared in over 50 silent movies between 1910 and 1932. She died in 1960 in Hollywood and has a star on the Hollywood Walk of Fame.

KATHLYN WILLIAMS
V. L. S. E. STAR

NEWSPAPER BOY DAVID MATTISON. David writes on November 17, 1906, "Dear Grandma and Grandpa I am selling papers now and I have made enough to buy a new suit, cap, mittens, suspenders, sweater, haircut and had my shoes half soled also a pair of drawers." Mattison, one of Butte's famous newspaper boys, is in many ways more impressive than Copper Kings Clark, Daly, and Heinze. He died in 1956 in Los Angeles, California.

1956 MIKE MANSFIELD CHRISTMAS POSTCARD. Mike Mansfield's Christmas postcards were drawn by his daughter Anne and sent to friends and constituents. Mansfield, born in New York City in 1903, served with the Marine Corps during World War I. He lived in Butte from 1922 to 1929 and worked as a mucker in Butte's copper mines. From 1943 to 1988, he was Montana's representative, a senator, senate majority leader, and ambassador to Japan. Mansfield never forgot his time and friends in Butte.

1958 MANSFIELD CHRISTMAS POSTCARD. Mike Mansfield said the "most influential person in his life" was his wife, Maureen, a high school teacher in Butte who persuaded him to go back to school. He briefly attended the Montana School of Mines and continued his education at the University of Montana in Missoula. His tombstone at Arlington National Cemetery simply lists his name, dates of birth and death, and "Pvt US Marine Corps."

LUIGI'S ONE-MAN BAND. Luigi (Ludvik Jurenic), a Serbian American, came to Butte in the 1930s, worked in the mines, left for a while, and came back to establish a tavern in Meaderville. He was famous for his 24-piece one-man band and dancing puppets, and for embarrassing customers coming from the restrooms. With the coming of the Berkeley Pit, he moved his establishment to 1826 Harrison Avenue. Luigi died at the age of 67 in 1984.

EDGAR S. PAXON. Edgar S. Paxon might be considered Butte's Charles M. Russell. He came to Montana in 1877 from New York and lived and painted in Butte from 1880 to 1906. This postcard portrays his masterpiece, *Custer's Last Stand*, painted at his studio on Woolman Street below the Steward mine. It took eight years to complete. The original painting is at the Buffalo Bill Historical Center in Cody, Wyoming.

"CUSTERS LAST STAND" BY EDGAR SAMUEL PAXON.

109515

BUFFALO HUNT. Paxon completed *Buffalo Hunt* in 1905. This painting also resides at the Buffalo Bill Historical Center. Paxon had no formal art training and began his career by painting theater sets for producer-manager John Maguire in Butte's Renshaw Hall on West Park Street and his other theaters in Butte and throughout Montana. He painted six historic scenes in the Montana Senate chamber and eight in the Missoula County Courthouse.

SELISH INDIAN
Flathead Indians are of the Selish Tribe, but were so called because they did not practice the Indian custom of deforming their heads. Their heads grew natural—flat on top. The Indian portrayed was named "Missoula".

SELISH INDIAN. Paxon produced a series of paintings of Native Americans of different tribes, some of which also were printed as postcards; this example is Missoula, a Montana Salish Indian (the name they prefer today). Paxon produced almost 2,000 paintings during his life, none bringing high prices. He received $1,000 for his eight murals in the Missoula County Courthouse. He died on November 9, 1919, in Missoula, where he had lived after 1906.

State Capitol, Helena, Mont.

AN-N-H!
YER FODDER'S MUSTACHE!

America's Foremost Comedienne

Martha Raye
at NICKY BLAIR'S
CARNIVAL

in The Hotel Capitol
51st St. at 8th Ave.
New York

FOR DINNER AT 8 — FOR SUPPER AT 12
SATURDAYS AND HOLIDAYS — 8, 10 AND 12

JOHN W. BONNER. This postcard of the state capitol in Helena was signed by John W. Bonner while governor in 1952. Bonner was born in Butte, received his law degree at the University of Montana in Missoula, and subsequently held various government positions. He resigned as attorney general of Montana in 1942 to enlist in the Army during World War II. He served as the 13th governor of Montana from 1949 to 1953.

COMEDIENNE MARTHA RAYE. Martha Raye was born Margy Reed at St. James Hospital in Butte in 1916. Her parents performed in vaudeville theater in Butte, and Martha and her brother joined the act. Martha was America's foremost comedienne in the 1940s and 1950s, appearing on radio, television, Broadway, and movies. She died in 1994 and has stars on the Hollywood Walk of Fame for both motion pictures and television.

Coxes Famous Army.

COXEY'S (HOGAN'S) ARMY. The silver price crash in 1893 led to a nationwide depression, and Jacob Coxey of Ohio organized protest marches on Washington, DC, to lobby for government jobs for the unemployed. A Montana contingent of about 500 men, organized by unemployed miner William Hogan of Butte, captured a Northern Pacific engine and cars on April 24, 1894, in Butte and headed east. They were stopped and arrested at Forsyth, Montana.

PALMER BROTHERS. The message reads: "There are two Palmer brothers and this is their business. They sit in the window of the P.O. News Stand and sell their cards . . . and I got one for you." No further information could be found on the Palmer brothers. The original Post Office News Stand was operated by brothers Luke and James Keefe from 1899 to 1929, and when this card was mailed in 1908, it was located at 27 West Park Street.

49

DR. CAROLINE MCGILL. Dr. McGill worked at Butte's Murray Hospital in 1911. She earned her medical degree at Johns Hopkins, returned to Butte in 1916, and practiced medicine at the Murray Hospital until retiring well-loved in 1956. She moved to her 320 Ranch in the Gallatin Canyon, donated many antiques to Montana State University, and helped establish the McGill Museum (one room is shown here), which became the Museum of the Rockies in 1965.

GABRIEL (TEDDY) TRAPARISH. "Mr. Meaderville" came to Butte in 1906 at the age of 19 from Dubrovnik, now part of Croatia. Eventually, he and two partners opened the Rocky Mountain Cafe in Meaderville. It became nationally famous during the 1930s for its meals and ambience. He reportedly bought a new Cadillac each year for almost 50 years. A lifelong bachelor, Teddy died on May 8, 1971, three weeks after buying his last Cadillac.

Four

Business and Advertising

Mining was the business of Butte, but the miners needed supporting service industries, and serving the miners was a lucrative business. These service industries employed more people than the mines and make up a big part of Butte's history. Providing food and clothing were perhaps the most necessary businesses, but so were the 250 or so saloons and the numerous brothels. Hotels and boardinghouses, restaurants and cafes, laundries, drugstores, blacksmiths, carriage and automobile sales and repair, newspaper and magazine stands, breweries, hardware stores, theaters, and many other types of businesses also made up the service industry of Butte.

The penny postcard was a common and relatively inexpensive method of advertising for businesses after the turn of the 20th century. Some were produced in large quantities, but many were produced in smaller quantities of 100–500, and some were just a few sent to friends by a proud business owner. Collecting advertising postcards is an underappreciated subspecialty, and many are uncommon or even rare. Advertising postcards portray part of the social and business history of a town, and many show interiors of buildings and exteriors of smaller businesses not otherwise seen in private or museum photograph collections. After the 1940s, motels were big users of advertising postcards. Only one motel postcard is shown in this chapter, but more are included in chapter five. Many smaller businesses are portrayed in this chapter; larger businesses are shown in chapter six.

One important Butte business not represented in these postcards is Town Pump. In 1953, Tom and Mary Kenneally started Town Pump in a small A-frame building next to the Butte Civic Center. Today, Town Pump is a large business owning more than 200 gas stations, convenience stores, and casinos in Montana.

Some businesses lasted for most of Butte's history, some occupied two to four different locations in Butte during their life, and some lasted no longer than a year or two. Enjoy some of the uncommon views, advertising jingles, messages, and history of Butte that follow.

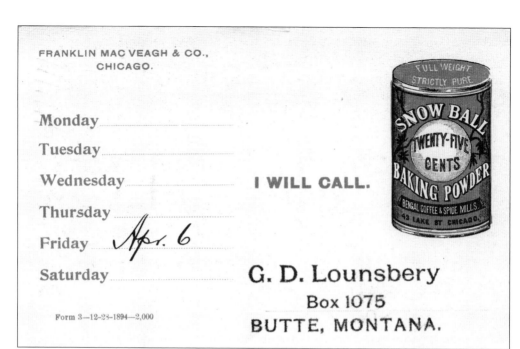

FRANKLIN MAC VEAGH & CO.,
CHICAGO.

Monday ....

Tuesday ....

Wednesday ....

Thursday ....

Friday *Apr. 6*

Saturday ....

I WILL CALL.

FULL WEIGHT
STRICTLY PURE

SNOW BALL
TWENTY-FIVE
CENTS
BAKING POWDER
BENGAL COFFEE & SPICE MILLS.
42 LAKE ST CHICAGO.

G. D. Lounsbery
Box 1075
BUTTE, MONTANA.

Form 3—12-23-1894—2,000

ADVERTISING BY SALESMEN. By the turn of the 20th century, Butte was becoming a regional center for distribution of goods by its businesses and for sales representatives from national companies. This government postal card advised S.R. Buford Company of Virginia City that G.D. Lounsbery of Butte, a representative for Snow Ball Baking Powder, would be arriving on April 6, 1900.

119—ANACONDA HILL—BUTTE, MONT.

BUTTE BREWING COMPANY. The Butte Brewing Company building can be seen at far left in this postcard. The company was started by German brewer Henry Muntzer in 1885. It was one of five breweries in Butte in the 1890s and survived until 1965. It was at the junction of Wyoming and Quartz Streets. Part of Finn Town is visible at right.

THE CHEQUAMEGON CAFE. This postcard shows the interior of the Chequamegon Dining Car, T.J. Casey, proprietor, at 19 North Main Street. This gentleman's restaurant was just north of the famous M&M and served workers and the wealthy. Others ran the cafe after Casey, and from the 1920s through 1954, its address was listed as 27 North Main Street. Locals called it "Chew Quick and Be Gone Again."

THE CREAMERY ANNEX. Theo McCabe and Roy McClelland came to Butte in 1903 and established the basement Creamery Cafe at 36 North Main Street. In 1913, a fire destroyed the location seen in this interior view, and they moved to 19 West Broadway Street. Their advertisements stated "Booths for Ladies" to let unescorted ladies know they would not be molested by men during their meal. The cafe operated until 1957.

The Chesapeake

36 North Main St.

Butte, Montana

Bessette-Casey Co.

THE CHESAPEAKE. This postcard for the Chesapeake was postmarked in 1910 and shows the same interior view as the Creamery Annex postcard. The location is also 36 North Main Street, so at some time before 1910, the Creamery Cafe may have been known as the Chesapeake. The message reads, "A good place to eat when you hit this town."

WHERE TO EAT WHEN IN BUTTE   PURITY CAFETERIA   22 W. BROADWAY, BUTTE, MONT.

PURITY CAFETERIA. The Purity Cafeteria at 22 West Broadway Street, pictured in 1916, was another example of Butte's early eating establishments. Both the postcard advertising and the message on back indicate "where to eat when in Butte." Although Butte was smoky, dirty, and dusty during peak mining years, note the beautiful white tablecloths provided for customers. Laundry bills were likely a big expense for this cafeteria.

ATLAS CAFE, 1914. A coffee and tea delivery truck is parked outside the Atlas Cafe. The Atlas Saloon and Restaurant at 81 East Park Street was listed in the Butte city directories from 1910 through 1918 under the restaurant category, indicating that serving food was its main business. To be competitive in Butte, serving drinks as well was advantageous. The license plate and "Westphal Photo Butte Mont" both indicate 1914 as the date of this postcard.

SYMONS ADVERTISING. This R.F. Outcault advertising postcard for Symons, featuring a June 1906 calendar and Buster Brown and Tige, was mailed on June 12, 1906; the new Symons department store opened in December 1906. Symons used another of its stores while rebuilding. In the early 1930s, Powder River Jack and Kitty Lee, a country music duo from Deer Lodge, sang their original advertising songs for Symons on the radio.

THE ARCADE BAR. This interior view of the Arcade, at the corner of Park and Main Streets, is from about 1930. The front reads, "This place has 10 bartenders working night and day." On the back is written, "This bar takes in $500 and $600 dollars a day. This is the place I am working this is one of the biggest gambling places in the west, $25,000 to 50,000 changes hands every day, never closes 24 hours a day." (Courtesy of David Perlstein.)

A.B.C. SALOON. This real-photo postcard of the A.B.C. Saloon's interior was sent to a friend in Belgium in 1906 by one of the proprietors (Victor). Located at the corner of Wyoming and Mercury Streets, this saloon in the brothel district received a visit by Carrie Nation in January 1910. She was allowed to give her anti-drinking speech and sent on her way. Victor's partner Lucian is at center against the bar. (Courtesy of Tom Mulvaney.)

NOBLE DRUG STORE. A.W. Noble (center) incorporated the Noble Drug Company in 1895. He sent this real-photo postcard to friends in 1913. A 1916 directory of druggists lists Noble Drug Store at 701 South Main Street, one of 31 drugstores in Butte. Butte had 10 post office substations by the 1920s, and a sign in the window indicates Noble's store was Substation No. 3. Noble's wife stands at right.

LISA CASH GROCERY COMPANY. This 1911 real-photo postcard shows the front window display for Lisa Cash Grocery at 107–109 East Park Street. Incorporated in 1899 by David Charles, Savin Lisa, and Martin Lisa, it specialized in wines imported from Germany, France, and Italy. Its retail location on East Park Street varied slightly over the years but it was still there in 1917. Its warehouse was at 401 Colorado Street. (Courtesy of Tom Mulvaney.)

LUTEY'S MARKETERIA. Joseph Lutey moved his grocery stores in Granite and Philipsburg, Montana, to Butte in 1897. With two sons, he established one of the largest retail and wholesale grocery stores in Montana. After Joseph's death in 1911, his sons established the nation's first self-serve grocery store in 1912. The Marketeria, at 142–144 West Park Street, was the business model for Piggly Wiggly, the nationwide self-service grocery chain established in 1916.

LUTEY'S ADVERTISING CALENDAR POSTCARD. In the year prior to converting to the self-service Marketeria, Lutey's grocery store used R.F. Outcault's comic strip characters Buster Brown (left) and his pit bull terrier Tige (right) to advertise "everything good to eat." The postcard was sent by a man in Feely, a town in Silver Bow County 10 miles north of Divide with no post office after 1904, to Marysville, Montana.

NEWBRO DRUG COMPANY. Dupont M. Newbro started a small retail drugstore in Butte in 1891. He became a wholesaler and distributed products throughout the United States. He also was president of the Washoe Copper Company but sold to Amalgamated Copper Company. In 1898, he invented Herpicide, a cure for dandruff. It became so successful that he sold his wholesale business and concentrated on selling Herpicide. His retail store was at 37 West Park Street.

MILLINERY ADVERTISING. Mary E. Hughes of 649 Utah Avenue sent this advertising postcard to a customer in Meaderville stating that her hat was not ready yet because the plume was still at the dyers. The year this postcard was mailed (1911) was the peak for the fashion of the very wide-brimmed hat pictured. Women's hats for everyday wear became less fashionable after World War II.

Yet not any nicer than your order for Peerless Tungsten, Tantalum, Gem, Miniature and Carbon Filament lamps would look to us. We have them all in stock.

MONTANA ELECTRIC COMPANY,
BUTTE, MONTANA.

MONTANA ELECTRIC COMPANY. This cowgirl advertises lamps for sale at the Montana Electric Company in 1909. The company is listed as a district sales office for the Westinghouse Company in 1916 and 1918 at 50–52 East Broadway Street in the Montana Electric Building. This building was also headquarters for Butte Electric & Power Company in 1911 before the two merged into the Montana Power Company.

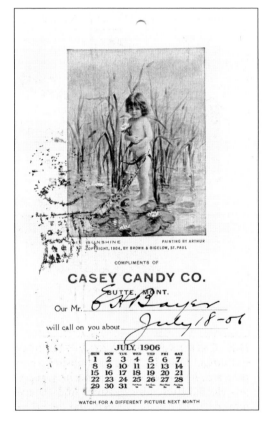

CASEY CANDY COMPANY. This hangable advertising postcard for Casey Candy Company featuring a July 1906 calendar was sent to Virginia City, Montana, merchant S.R. Buford to announce the arrival date of Casey's salesman. Casey Candy Company was at 15–19 East Silver Street from at least 1906 to 1918. Frank Casey was president until 1918, when Alonzo Patterson took over. Mon-Ta-Na Chocolates were a specialty gift "when words and letters fail," as the company advertised.

I. MATTINGLY, MEN'S FURNISHINGS. Calendar postcards for business advertising were popular in the early 1900s. Located at 117 North Main Street, this business was originally Smith & Mattingly in the 1890s and early 1900s. By 1913, Mattingly was the sole owner, and the message on the back advertised both men's and women's Phoenix hosiery. Today, the Mattingly location is home to Old Butte Historical Adventures.

B.E. CALKINS ADVERTISING POSTCARD. Benjamin Elmer Calkins owned a small bookstore in Butte in 1886. In 1898, he published a book with 86 scenes of Butte. By the time of this 1905 postcard, he had expanded to business supplies and moved to Main and Broadway Streets. He was elected Butte city treasurer in 1901 and was the only Republican elected in the city. He moved to Los Angeles in 1919 and died there in 1939.

CORNER of Flower Garden of the Sorosis Annex, a Club House maintained at Lynn, Massachusetts, by the manufacturers of Sorosis Shoes for the comfort and recreation of their Women employees.

SOROSIS SHOES
sold by
M. J. Connell Co.
Butte, Mont.

M.J. CONNELL COMPANY ADVERTISING. Advertising Sorosis shoes, this 1908 puzzle postcard was designed to be cut into pieces according to instructions on the back, mailed in an envelope, and reconstructed by the recipient. Connell came to Montana in 1875 and engaged in many mercantile enterprises. He sold the M.J. Connell Company (which merged with Hennessy's in 1926) and other businesses and moved to California a very rich man.

ALLEN & DARNELL TAILORS. "Who's" Allen and "Why" Darnell were tailors who operated a men's clothing store at 207 East Park Street from about 1900 into the 1920s. This real-photo postcard of their whitewashed rock advertisement (estimated as more than 300 feet long by the photographer) on Test Hill was taken by "Will" in 1910 and sent to a lady friend in Detroit, Michigan. The caption on back reads, "Toward Columbia Gardens."

CAVILL'S TRAINING SCHOOL FOR DOGS. Joseph R. Cavill, born in Wisconsin in 1887, engaged in a variety of jobs throughout his life. By the 1930 census and in the 1934 Butte city directory, he was living in Butte, and his occupation was dog trainer at 2131 Harvard Avenue. He was in Butte but no longer a dog trainer in the 1940 census. Cavill died at the age of 80 in Los Angeles in 1967.

BUTTE CARRIAGE WORKS. This advertising postcard for Butte Carriage Works represents its last years in business in the late 1930s–early 1940s. It started on South Main Street in the mid-1890s as a carriage and wagon maker and also a blacksmith shop, shoeing up to 30 horses per day. After several moves, the business was on Silver Street, and by 1917, it had started concentrating on autobody repair for the automobiles that were replacing horses.

IT IS OFTEN GREATER ECONOMY
—to have damaged automobile fenders or bodies repainted, or repaired, before "old man" rust gets at them.
We use the 3-M System for this work and shall be pleased to give you an estimate of the actual cost—without obligation.

BUTTE CARRIAGE WORKS, Inc.
38 to 48 E. Silver St.
Butte, Montana

OLYMPIAN SERVICE STATION. This late-1930s advertising postcard for the Olympian Service Station features Richfield gasoline. Richfield had just emerged from bankruptcy. In 1942, two of its oil tanks near Santa Barbara, California, were bombarded by the Japanese in the first attack on the continental United States in World War II. This Richfield service station in Butte was at 935 South Montana Street near the Milwaukee Railroad depot.

SOUTH SIDE HARDWARE SANTA LETTERS. In 1939, South Side Hardware moved to the old Harrison Avenue Theatre building, which had been open since 1917. This postcard indicates that in the 1940s–1950s, it had a "letter to Santa" program for the children of Butte that was intended to bring in their parents for Christmas shopping. South Side Hardware remained at 1803 Harrison Avenue until 1997. Great Harvest Bread located there in 2001.

We have received the letter you wrote to Santa Claus and have checked the items you would like to have for Christmas. We have them and others and invite you to see them at our store.

Present this card at our store and you will receive a gift.

South Side Hardware

 2

BUTTE, MARCH 11, 1937

Campbell's SOUPS

TOMATO

The Most Popular Soup in the World

Special Price

3 Cans for 25 Cents——95 Cents Per Dozen

Tune in on "Hollywood Hotel"—broadcast over Radio Station KSL every Friday evening at 7:00 o'clock. Also Burns and Allen each Wednesday at 9:30 P. M.

CARL'S GROCERY AND MEATS

1827 SO. MONTANA ST.   PHONE 2-1520

CARL'S GROCERY AND MEATS. In March 1937, Carl's Grocery and Meats used a "Campbell Kids" postcard to advertise Campbell's tomato soup for as low as 8¢ per can when purchased by the dozen. Its advertising included sponsoring two weekly programs on radio station KSL, *Hollywood Hotel* and *Burns and Allen.* Carl's was at 1827 South Montana Street, now the location of the Montana Street overpass for Interstate 90.

BOARD OF TRADE. This 1930s real-photo postcard shows the second Board of Trade saloon at 16–18 East Park Street, opened in 1917 two buildings east of the Rialto Theater. The writing on the central pillar reads, "Through our Doors Pass the Nicest People in the World—Our Customers." Note the advertising for Camel cigarettes.

BOARD OF TRADE INTERIOR, 1930s. On June 8, 1959, Ruby Garrett, the last madam of the last brothel in Butte, the Dumas, shot and killed her common-law husband, Andy Arrigoni, in the Board of Trade, citing continued physical abuse. When the Rialto was demolished in 1965, the Board of Trade moved to East Broadway Street. It was destroyed by fire in 1969.

GREEN'S CAFE, 1920s. This real-photo postcard was likely produced as advertising for Green's Cafe. Hi (Hiram) and Jack Lloyd owned and ran Green's Cafe at 43 North Main Street in Butte in the 1920s and 1930s. It was billed as the place "where men meet and eat." A photographer is standing on top of the automobile at this special event, and only two women can be seen.

EDDY'S MOTEL. Jack Lloyd, formerly a co-owner of Green's Cafe, purchased Eddy's Motel at 1205 South Montana Street in 1945 and added a cocktail lounge to an associated restaurant at 1201 South Montana Street. Eddy's was one of the early Butte motels serving increased automobile traffic. It remains in business in 2020.

LLOYD'S OF BUTTE, 1940s. Jack Lloyd purchased Eddy's Motel and associated restaurant, idle during the war years, from former Butte mayor Archie McTaggart and spent approximately $75,000 on renovations, primarily to the restaurant and the addition of a cocktail lounge. The end of gasoline rationing and increasing travel after World War II made this purchase and renovation a timely investment.

LLOYD'S OF BUTTE, 1950s. Lloyd's of Butte became one of the largest entertainment centers in the city. It advertised "Lloyd's of Butte—Not of London—Insures You Good Food." There was a regular dining room, a cocktail lounge, and additional banquet rooms. The 4-Bs Cafe occupied the building during the 1960s and 1970s. The building still exists and has housed a restaurant and casino.

MEADERVILLE AND THE ROCKY MOUNTAIN CAFE. The largest white building in the center of this 1938–1939 real-photo postcard is Teddy Traparish's famous Rocky Mountain Cafe. Within were a dance floor, a gambling room, a bar, and a dining room. Its meals became nationally famous, and author and reviewer John Gunther wrote, "The steaks are 7 inches thick and cover half an acre." A fire on July 2, 1940, destroyed this building.

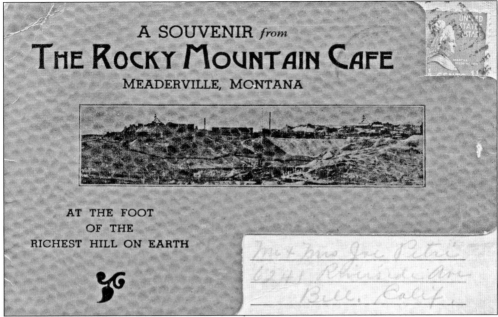

ROCKY MOUNTAIN CAFE ADVERTISING POSTCARD. This 1940s advertising postcard touted the splendors of Meaderville and Butte. In addition to steaks, large hors d'oeuvres trays and Italian food were specialties. After the 1940 fire, the restaurant was re-established just down the street. The expanding Berkeley Pit resulted in Teddy Traparish closing in 1961, and in 1966, he donated the back bar to the World Museum of Mining. It is now on loan to Headframe Spirits Distillery.

ARO CAFE, MEADERVILLE. The Aro Cafe, three doors down from the Rocky Mountain Cafe, was another famous eating place in Meaderville. Fred's Place (Meaderville Pool Hall) and a small Victorian residence were between the two restaurants. This postcard shows an interior view of the Aro. The back of the card advertises chicken, steaks, and ravioli. The exterior sign was in the shape of an arrow. (Courtesy of Tom Mulvaney.)

HUNTER'S COPPER GIFT AND MAGIC STORE. The store featured in this real-photo advertising postcard started as a cigar store at 46 North Main Street operated by William Henry Hunter in the early 1950s. By 1956, it sold copper gifts, jewelry, and magic tricks. After a divorce in 1960, the store closed. Later, Kitty's and the Butte Copper Company, both on Harrison Avenue, sold gifts made of copper. The Butte Copper Company continues in business.

FRED AND MILLIE'S CAFE. This early-1960s postcard shows Fred R. and Mildred Kalamaha's cafe and lounge at 3525 Harrison Avenue. Fred and Millie's operated from 1961 to 1978. At some time during the 1960s, this business was owned by Phyllis Sutey, whose son Dave established the Thriftway Super Stops chain of service stations and convenience stores in Montana. The Bank of Butte was at this location in 2020.

Five

TRANSPORTATION
AND TRAVEL

Until 1880, transportation in Montana Territory was by foot, horse and mule, or horse-drawn conveyances. For years, the citizens of Montana Territory had hoped for railroads, because receiving supplies and equipment and shipping mining, agricultural, and other products out of the territory was time consuming and costly. On May 9, 1880, the Utah & Northern Railway crossed into Montana, and by October 1881, it was at the town of Silver Bow, just west of Butte. On December 21, 1881, the first train rolled into Butte.

The Utah & Northern connected with the newly completed Northern Pacific tracks at Garrison Junction on September 23, 1883. In 1886, the Utah & Northern and Northern Pacific Railroads formed the cooperative Montana Union to run trains and freight from Garrison Junction to Butte. The Montana Central Branch of the Great Northern Railroad reached Butte in 1888. In 1892, tired of excessive freight rates on the Montana Union, Marcus Daly initiated his own railroad, the Butte, Anaconda & Pacific Railway, to carry ore from Butte to his smelter in Anaconda. By 1909, the Chicago, Milwaukee & St. Paul Railroad had tracks through Butte, which was now served by three transcontinental lines and one local railroad. Construction of the Northern Pacific Butte Short Line from Logan over Pipestone Pass to Butte was completed in late March 1890. Butte became the center of railroad transportation in Montana.

With the coming of the automobile, transportation and business models changed dramatically. The *Butte Inter Mountain* reported that on July 12, 1902, four Butte citizens owned "experimental" automobiles. Butte's E.C. Largey was the first in Montana to register an automobile with the secretary of state after new legislation in 1913. By 1916, automobiles were more common in Montana, and by the late 1920s, they were widely owned.

The building of better and widespread routes (later highways) for travelers in automobiles became important, as did overnight accommodations. The first Montana camping grounds and tourist courts were built in the mid-1920s. The first motel was in San Luis Obispo, California, in 1925. In April 1939, the Westward Ho Motel in Billings was the first motel mentioned in Montana newspapers.

A SIXTEEN HORSE ORE TEAM. BUTTE, MONT.

EARLY ORE TRANSPORTATION. Prior to electric rail lines, ore had to be hauled from mine shafts to smelters by horse or mule teams. The ore wagon drawn by a 16-horse team pictured here was only cost efficient with the highest-quality ores. The original photograph for this postcard likely dates from the silver mining period of the 1870s–1880s. (Courtesy of Tom Mulvaney.)

1067 – NORTHERN PACIFIC DEPOT, BUTTE, MONTANA.

NORTHERN PACIFIC RAILROAD DEPOT. The Northern Pacific depot at 800 East Front Street in Butte was completed in 1906 and used by the Northern Pacific and the Utah & Northern (later Union Pacific's Oregon Short Line) Railroads. Many US presidents and celebrities passed through this depot over the years. Last used as an Amtrak station in 1979, it has been restored and is now an events center.

"TAP 'ER LIGHT." This 1940s advertising postcard for Butte, handed out by American Women's Voluntary Services at the Northern Pacific depot, was intended for status updates to homefolks by servicemen. Other services included stationery, magazines, coffee, snacks, and a friendly ear. Almost all Montana men enlisting for service in World War II embarked from Butte. "Tap 'er Light" is a miners' expression meaning don't tamp the dynamite in too hard, or "take it easy,"

GREAT NORTHERN RAILROAD DEPOT. The Great Northern was the second major railroad to reach Butte, but the depot in this postcard was not built until 1916. Passenger service stopped in the late 1960s, and since then, the building at 818 South Arizona Avenue was used by a number of businesses. It was vacant in 2020.

CHICAGO, MILWAUKEE & ST. PAUL DEPOT AND TRAIN SHEDS, BUTTE, MONT.

CHICAGO, MILWAUKEE & ST. PAUL DEPOT. The Chicago, Milwaukee & St. Paul Railway was the last transcontinental railroad to reach Butte. The depot in this postcard was built in 1916. The building at 1003 South Montana Street, with its soaring clock tower, is a landmark and has served as the headquarters for KXLF television for many years.

BAP DEPOT   BUTTE, MONTANA

BUTTE, ANACONDA & PACIFIC DEPOT. The Butte, Anaconda & Pacific (BA&P) Railroad was completed in 1893 to carry Marcus Daly's copper ore to his smelter at Anaconda. As a common carrier, BA&P also carried some passengers and general freight. The depot in Butte was built in 1895 as separate passenger and freight depots and combined in 1898. This postcard features the passenger (east) depot, which was on Utah Avenue and was demolished after 1985.

Train Load of Copper Ore, Butte, Montana   30835-N

MOVING COPPER ORE BY TRAIN. Marcus Daly established Anaconda, built his smelter there, and built the BA&P to convey the ore from Butte mines to the smelter. With only 26 miles of mainline and 135 miles total, BA&P was called the "Biggest Little Railroad in the Nation." It converted from steam to electric in 1913, the first heavy freight railroad in the country to do so.

BUTTE, ANACONDA & PACIFIC ORE TRAIN. This real-photo postcard from the early 1950s shows a long BA&P ore train headed to the Anaconda smelter from Butte. The Northern Pacific Railroad tracks are those with the small bridge at center. The Chicago, Milwaukee & Pacific tracks are nearest the cliff at left and center.

75

APPROACHING BUTTE, MONT. ON NORTHERN PACIFIC R. R.

BUTTE-BOUND NORTHERN PACIFIC SHORT LINE. The train pictured here about 1908–1910 is approaching Homestake at the Continental Divide. At Homestake, the helper engine at the rear of the train was removed and sent back to Whitehall, and the train then traveled downhill to Butte. To celebrate the opening of the Northern Pacific Short Line in late May 1890, special excursion trains went from Bozeman to Butte and from Butte to Bozeman on the Butte–Gallatin Branch.

SEEING BUTTE OBSERVATION CAR. As part of W.A. Clark's Butte Electric Railway Company, the Seeing Butte Observation Car was started in the early 1900s to attract tourists such as these viewing the West Steward mine. The labor troubles of 1914–1917 and World War I resulted in a dramatic decline in tourism, and the Seeing Butte Observation Car experiment was discontinued.

Scene in Business District, Seeing Butte Car, Butte, Mont.

BUTTE ELECTRIC RAILWAY. The observation car was a short-term experiment, but in 1910, the regular electric trolly routes included 49 cars and 33 miles of track. One very important function of the cars for Butte's citizens and children was low-cost transportation to Clark's Columbia Gardens. The Anaconda Copper Mining Company acquired the Butte Electric Railway Company in 1928, and it operated through 1937, when buses began replacing the trolley cars.

Ore Conveying by Electricity, BUTTE, Mont.

ELECTRIC ORE CARS. Increasing electrification of the mines changed lighting, hoisting, and drilling methods. By the 1910s, electrification also resulted in some small mines conveying ore by electric car to nearby smelters. For a while, these small electric cars carried ore over Butte Electric Railway tracks through downtown Butte to W.A. Clark's smelters. Most shipments of ore were by the large BA&P trains to Anaconda.

SKOOKUM KABIN KAMP. Opened in 1926 at 3535–3541 Harrison Avenue, Skookum was one of the first tourist camps and service stations opened in Montana for the increasing automobile tourists. It was operated for many years by the Howes family and was sold to the Miller family in 1946. It operated until the early 1990s, was torn down in 2015, and in 2020 is the site of Pizza Ranch.

COOK'S CABIN CAMP. Grocer Leonard Cook and his wife, Jane, opened Cook's Cabin Camp in 1929 at 1405 Dewey Boulevard. As the use of automobiles increased, hotels declined in importance, and this precursor to the motel industry had small cabins, a convenience store, and a gasoline pump. Operation was taken over by the Harding family in 1946 and was scaled back to only a grocery store in the 1960s. It closed around 1980.

Mile-Hi Motel — in city limits, Butte, Mont.
32 Rooms

MILE-HI MOTEL. Located at 3499 Harrison Avenue, the Mile-Hi was a second-generation accommodation for tourists. The term "motel" first appears in Montana about 1939. The Mile-Hi was managed by Frank and Irene Snell from 1948 through the early 1960s. It had a new and distinctive coat of light blue paint by 1968. In 2020, the Hampton Inn occupies the former site of the Mile-Hi Motel.

MARY LOU MOTEL. The Mary Lou Motel, at 3219 Harrison Avenue, was another of the second generation of accommodations for tourists clustered on Harrison Avenue (Highway 10) at the southern entrance to Butte. Lewis and Mary Graham built the motel in 1952 and named it after their granddaughter. They also started the adjacent Raymond's Fireside Lounge and Supper Club, known for its smorgasbord.

214 POINT OF ROCKS ON HARDING WAY, NEAR BUTTE.

ON YELLOWSTONE TRAIL

HARDING WAY. Originally known as Highway 10 and part of the Yellowstone Trail, this highway over Pipestone Pass was built in 1926 and named in honor of Pres. Warren Harding's visit to Butte in 1923. It became a major entrance to Butte and is still used today as a scenic alternative to Interstate 90. Two water fountains on the route were used by travelers for a cool drink and to refill radiators of overheated automobiles.

SILVER BOW COUNTY AIRPORT. The Butte Municipal Airport was established in 1926, and the name was changed to Silver Bow County Airport from 1960 to 1972. This postcard shows the Swiss chalet–style terminal of the late 1960s. In 1972, the name was changed to the Bert Mooney airport to honor the Butte aviator who was the first to fly mail to Yellowstone National Park in 1935. A new terminal was completed in 2018.

Six

STREETS, OVERVIEWS, AND BUILDINGS

At least partially because of its date of establishment, mercantile importance, and population size, Butte has a late-19th and early-20th century architectural character not seen in other Montana towns. The Butte-Anaconda National Historic District, the largest in the United States, was established in 1961. Within the Butte portion of the district, the area between Main and Montana Streets and Park and Broadway Streets comprises the bulk of the primary historic business buildings, though more than 4,000 historic buildings, including small miners' cottages, are included within the total area. Many of these buildings have been saved, but hundreds have been lost since the historic district was created. Cost of renovation and a declining population base leading to economic decline have hindered preservation. Many original buildings were destroyed by numerous fires over the years. Other early buildings were demolished to erect newer and larger buildings during the building boom of 1905–1920. Postcards produced during this period document the location and physical appearance of some of these lost buildings.

Images and photographs on postcards usually concentrated on what were considered at the time the most important buildings and scenes. However, many postcards show other buildings and scenes that are missing from today's landscape. Landscape views of early Butte show clearly how mines, businesses, and miners' housing closely intertwined with each other in north Butte (or the Butte Hill). Comparison of early and later street views on postcards also document both stability and changes of businesses and buildings over the years. Thus, postcard views are an important part of Butte's architectural and business history.

The collection of postcards in this chapter displays the character of the streets of the old central business district, some of the unique architecture in Butte preserved to this day, some unique buildings lost, and the inseparability of Butte's mines, businesses, and working citizens. Also presented are brief histories of the buildings, businesses, and associated personalities related to the scenes. May the historic preservation of unique Butte continue.

NORTH BUTTE PANORAMA, 1908. This trifold postcard from about 1908 shows Hotel Pleasonton at far left and the federal courthouse on the horizon above it. Near the fold to the right is the gallows frame for the Steward mine. Wyoming Street is at center, with the Dorothy Apartments

NORTH BUTTE PANORAMA, 1961. This five-fold panorama postcard from about 1961 shows the Hirbour Tower and Hennessy's on the left and Arizona Street at center. The curved street to the right of Arizona Street is Covert Street; along with East Broadway and East Park Streets

at bottom center and the Butte Brewery behind them. The Washoe mine is just above and to the right of the Dorothy Apartments.

at far right, this comprised much of Finn Town. Some of the multicultural Eastside is on the right edge of the postcard.

ORIGINAL FINLEN HOTEL. The original Finlen Hotel (left), pictured around 1910, hosted many local and national dignitaries. Butte grew rapidly from 1880 to 1890, and in 1889, a new three-story hotel called the McDermott was built on the southeast corner of East Broadway and Wyoming Streets. Mining entrepreneur Miles Finlen purchased the hotel and renamed it the Finlen in the late 1890s. The Thornton Hotel is on the right.

LOBBY OF ORIGINAL FINLEN. Guests could buy cigars and postcards in the luxurious lobby of the original Finlen Hotel. It is likely that both this postcard and the preceding one were in the postcard rack on the far left. Miles Finlen moved to New York, and his son James operated the hotel from the early 1900s through 1923, when he rebuilt it.

NEW FINLEN HOTEL. The New Finlen Hotel, modeled after the Hotel Astor in New York City, opened in January 1924. It had nine stories and 250 rooms and hosted Thomas Edison, Charles Lindbergh, John F. Kennedy, and Richard Nixon, among other dignitaries. A motor inn was added in the 1950s. The Finlen is one of Butte's few original hotels still operating.

New Finlen Hotel, Butte, Mont.   97553-N

THE THORNTON HOTEL. The original Thornton Hotel was built in 1890. In 1901, the five-story Thornton Block (and hotel) was built adjoining on the east, at 65 East Broadway Street. In 1914, Jeanette Rankin's Montana Equal Suffrage Association office occupied room 207. In 1916, Rankin became the first woman elected to the US House of Representatives.

Thornton Hotel, Butte, Mont.

Anaconda Copper Mining Co. Employees Club, Butte, Mont.

ANACONDA COMPANY EMPLOYEES CLUB. Other luminaries stayed at the Thornton over the years, including Booker T. Washington in 1913. Teddy Roosevelt attended a banquet there in 1903. The Thornton ceased to be a hotel and was used by the Anaconda Copper Mining Company as a club for its employees and spouses after 1947.

Snack Bar
Anaconda Copper Mining Co. Employees Club, Butte, Mont.

ACM EMPLOYEES CLUB SNACK BAR. In addition to a main and women's lounge, the club had a snack bar, bowling alley, dance floor, and other rooms for recreation and meetings. Both the original Thornton Hotel and the Thornton Block survive, and now serve as an office building with some businesses on the ground floor.

Hennessy's Big Store in Butte
The Annex in the Rear Contains
The Finest Grocery
and Meat Market
in the Northwest

HENNESSY'S. Butte's most famous and elegant department store and building opened in 1898. Marcus Daly provided financial support to Daniel Hennessy to compete with Daly's former associate A.B. Hammond, who owned the Missoula Mercantile. In 1901, the ACM moved its executive offices to the sixth floor. The building remains, but Hennessy's of Butte closed in 1980.

Part of the Residence District, Butte, Mont.

HENNESSY AND KELLEY MANSIONS. Daniel Hennessy's success allowed him to build one of Butte's most elegant mansions (left, at West Park Street and Excelsior Avenue). His neighbor to the east (right), Cornelius "Con" Kelley, was the longtime president (1918–1940) and chairman of the board (1940–1955) of the ACM. This westside neighborhood was also home to many businessmen and professionals.

NEW SYMONS BLOCK. Hennessy's largest competitor in Butte was Symons Dry Goods Company. Symons was founded by William and Harry Symons and two members of the Oppenheimer family in 1897. The large Butte fire of September 1905 destroyed the Symons store, and a new building rose from the ashes in 1906. It was called the Phoenix Block (or Symons on this postcard) and contained the new Symons store.

OWSLEY BLOCK. The Owsley Block, finished in 1892, was owned by William Owsley, mayor of Butte from 1882 to 1885. On the northeast corner of Park and Main Streets, it contained numerous businesses on the ground floor, offices on other floors, and the Butte Business College on the sixth (top) floor. In later years, it was called the Medical Arts Building. It was destroyed by fire in 1973. In 2020, the new Northwest Energy building occupied the site.

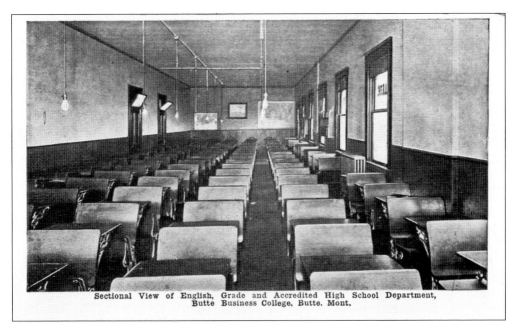

Sectional View of English, Grade and Accredited High School Department,
Butte Business College, Butte, Mont.

BUTTE BUSINESS COLLEGE. This postcard view shows a classroom at the Butte Business College on the sixth floor of the Owsley Block. By 1916, it was the seventh largest commercial college in the United States, with 10,000 graduates, 800 daily attendees, and 14 teachers in three shifts. Business courses such as shorthand and bookkeeping were important, but it also had elementary and high school classes and importantly, taught English to numerous immigrant miners.

THE ACOMA HOTEL. Butte had many large hotels and also smaller hotels like the Acoma. The coming of the automobile, tourist camps, and the first motels reduced their importance. Smaller hotels such as the Acoma, even in their prime, often served as residence hotels, with rates by the week or month. The Acoma, including a bar and restaurant, is on the southwest corner of East Broadway and Wyoming Streets near the Finlen Hotel.

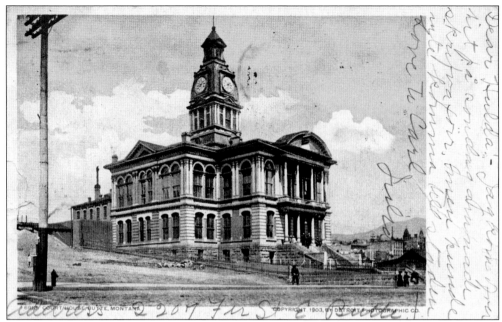

FIRST SILVER BOW COUNTY COURTHOUSE. As silver mining increased the population and wealth of Butte, Silver Bow County was established in 1881 from the southern part of Deer Lodge County. By late 1882, a substantial county courthouse, pictured on this 1903 postcard, was built. By 1910, this first courthouse was considered dilapidated, and it was torn down, with a new courthouse completed in 1912 on the same site.

NEW COURTHOUSE, 1912. Silver Bow County's new Beaux-Arts–style courthouse at 155 West Granite Street was dedicated on July 4, 1912. Its cost rivaled that of the state capitol in Helena, and its attractive interior is worth a visit. The courthouse served as a barracks for troops sent to Butte to quell labor unrest following the 1914 dynamiting of the Miner's Union Hall. Franklin Roosevelt gave political speeches here in 1920 and 1932.

STATE SAVINGS BANK. Also known as Metals Bank, this building was designed by Cass Gilbert and constructed in 1906 at 8 West Park Street. F.A. Heinze was a director and the largest stockholder of the bank, and E.P. Chapin managed it. Chapin had many battles with architect Gilbert in building the bank. The building is now owned by the Ueland family and contains the Metals Sports Bar and Grill.

BUTTE CIVIC CENTER. The doors to the civic center opened in 1952. It has since accommodated millions of people with numerous events such as the Ringling Brothers circus, many Montana sports tournaments, home and trade shows, graduations, public ice skating, rodeos, boxing, and major entertainers such as the Beach Boys and Holiday on Ice. Since 1987, it has also been the home of the Butte Sports Hall of Fame.

SISTER'S HOSPITAL. Sister's Hospital, also known as St. James Community Hospital, one of Butte's earliest hospitals, was started in 1881 by five sisters from the Sisters of Charity. The sisters quickly raised a large amount of money, because a hospital was a popular cause and was needed. Additions and improvements were made in 1889, 1895, 1906 (a nursing school), 1915, and the 1940s. St. James Health Care continues service to Butte today.

MURRAY HOSPITAL. Dr. Thomas J. Murray came to Butte in 1885, and in 1886, he and Dr. Robert L. Gillespie built the Murray and Gillespie Hospital. In 1894, it became the Murray and Freund Hospital, and in 1906, it became the Murray Hospital. Dr. Murray was prominent not only in Butte but nationally as well. He died in 1930. The hospital was at the corner of Quartz and Alaska Streets and is a parking lot today.

Y.M.C.A. BUILDING, BUTTE, MONT.

85769

YMCA BUILDING. The YMCA building at 405 West Park Street opened in 1919. It was built with a goal to help educate and improve the life of the working class. There were separate entrances for boys and men. The Butte–Silver Bow Arts Foundation bought the building in 2005 for $1 and occupied it until 2013, when overhead costs became too high to continue. The building is still in private ownership but was unoccupied as of 2020.

12613. Federal Bldg., Butte, Mont.

FEDERAL COURTHOUSE AND POST OFFICE. The federal building and post office at 400 North Main Street was dedicated on December 8, 1904, and expanded in 1933–1934. Its courtroom was the site for naturalization ceremonies for thousands of immigrants. The post office moved out in 1965, and in 2002, the building was renamed the Mike Mansfield Federal Building and US Courthouse.

HIRBOUR BLOCK, BUTTE, MONT.

NO. 7

KNIGHTS OF COLUMBUS BUILDING. The Butte Knights of Columbus No. 68, a Catholic fraternal organization, formed in 1902 and constructed a three-story building in 1917 at 224 West Park Street. Through the years, they have conducted many community events, banquets, dances, and fundraisers for local charities (101 events in 2016 alone). Additionally, their building is home to Butte's Sports Picture Gallery, which by itself is well worth a visit.

THE HIRBOUR TOWER. The Hirbour Tower, built in 1901, was the second skyscraper built west of the Mississippi River (San Francisco had the first). Although eight stories might not seem enough to qualify for the name, a skyscraper is defined by having an internal vertical steel girder structure rather than brick or concrete. The building was unoccupied in 2010 but was purchased and converted to residences and a variety of businesses by 2015.

BUTTE PUBLIC LIBRARY. The Butte Public Library opened in 1894 at 106 West Broadway Street. "Mr. Montana" Granville Stuart was head librarian from 1905 through 1914. In September 1905, a fire spread from Symon's Dry Goods, damaging the library. In March 1960, a fire damaged the library so severely that only the first floor and basement were salvaged. A new library opened in October 1991 at 226 West Broadway Street.

PUBLIC LIBRARY, BUTTE, MONT.   NO. 59

12 Masonic Temple, Butte, Mont.

THE MASONIC TEMPLE. Butte's Masonic temple was constructed at 314 West Park Street in 1902 in the Beaux-Arts style. In 1922, the Masons erected a new building immediately adjacent, but because of declining membership, they never occupied it. Fox Film Company leased the new building from the 1920s to the 1980s, and it became the Fox Theater. It is now the Mother Lode Theatre. The Masons still occupy the original building.

GRANITE ST., LOOKING WEST, SHOWING IND. TELEPHONE AND SILVER BOW CLUB BUILDINGS, BUTTE, MONT.

NO. 33

GRANITE STREET LOOKING WEST. This view of Granite Street shows the old Silver Bow Club (right), a gentleman's club for Butte's elite; the building was completed in 1907. Beginning in the 1940s, it housed the Butte Miner's Union offices. A small portion of the old courthouse is visible just beyond the Silver Bow Club. The building on the left with columns was the old Independent Telephone Company, now the Butte Water Company.

12620. East from Hennessy's, Butte, Mont.

WYOMING AND GRANITE STREET INTERSECTION. The Dorothy Apartments (rooming house) is the large building at left on the northeast corner of Wyoming and Granite Streets. Butte Brewery is on the left edge, and millionaire John Noyes's house is at the very bottom left corner of this postcard. Noyes made some money in mining, but most of his millions were from real estate development. None of these buildings survive.

NORTH MAIN STREET, SEPTEMBER 2, 1907. The statue at the center of Main Street honoring Copper King Marcus Daly was unveiled on Labor Day, September 2, 1907. Undoubtably, both before and after the ceremony, a few of the many spectators pictured in this scene visited the Washoe Saloon (far left with American flag) to have a glass or two of the Eureka beer it advertised, produced by the Butte Brewing Company.

1068 — UNVEILING MARCUS DALY MONUMENT, LABOR DAY, BUTTE, MONTANA

HARRISON AVENUE, LATE 1960s. The Butte Plaza Mall, built in 1966 at 3100 Harrison Avenue, is at the center of this late-1960s aerial view of Harrison Avenue looking north. The Butte Country Club is at right center, and the south Harrison Avenue corridor is lightly developed compared to today. The mall, like many other malls across the country, has seen the loss of anchor stores and is struggling compared to its early years.

CENTERVILLE, CORKTOWN, AND DUBLIN GULCH. The gallows frame for the West Steward mine is at far left on the left panel of this two-panel postcard with some of the town of Walkerville behind it. A portion of Centerville fills the remainder of the left panel, and the original St. Mary's (Irish Catholic) Church is at center. This original St. Mary's Church, on North Wyoming Street,

burned in August 1931. On the right panel, the seven stacks of the Neversweat mine are at far right, the Parrot mine is below that, and the Kelley mine (Butte's last operating underground mine) is at center, to the left of the Anaconda Road. Also to the left of the Anaconda Road are the Irish communities of Dublin Gulch, Corktown, and Muckerville.

View of Butte, Mont., with Main Range of Rockies in Distance. 41.

VIEW OF SOUTHEAST BUTTE. This postcard aerial view of southeast Butte shows East Park Street at bottom left. Portions of East Galena and East Mercury Streets are to the right of Park Street. South Arizona Street runs from the Silver Queen Furnished Rooms building (with the "Overland Rye cures the blues" sign at far left) to the middle right edge of the postcard.

245 — WEST PARK STREET, BUTTE, MONTANA.

WEST PARK STREET FROM MAIN STREET. The Lizzie Block (gone by about 1957), at the corner of Park and Main Streets, is at far right in this 1908 view. The Lizzie Block was home to a number of businesses, including the Arcade Bar. The next building west with the turret is the Curtis Music Hall, which still stands. Gamers Cafe is on the ground floor of the Curtis Music Hall.

Park Street, Looking West, Showing Big Butte, Butte, Mont.

PARK STREET LOOKING WEST, 1910. The tall building with the Savings Bank sign is the Clark Hotel. The Boucher clothing store, with four upper-story windows, is at bottom right. Frank Boucher came to Butte in 1879 and worked as a woodcutter and blacksmith and in the livery business before establishing a successful clothing store. In 1926, he also owned the Victoria Hotel and rooming house at 11 East Mercury Street.

Park Street, Looking West, Butte, Montana

PARK STREET LOOKING WEST, 1940s. The building with the Prudential Savings sign is the Clark Hotel, and across Park Street on the left is the Symons mercantile. A fire in 1972 destroyed the Clark Hotel, the J.C. Penney building just west of the Clark Hotel, and 11 other businesses in this scene. In the far distance at center with the triangular sign on top is the YMCA building, constructed in 1919.

MAIN STREET LOOKING NORTH, 1909. In this view of Main Street looking north from Park Street, the Lizzie Block is on the left, and the Owsley Block is on the right. Near the center is the Hirbour Tower on the northeast corner of Main and Broadway Streets, and behind it is the Hennessy building. The sign on the front of the streetcar advertises a baseball game.

BUSY PARK AND MAIN STREETS, 1909. At far left in this slightly different view of Main Street looking north is the Lizzie Block, which contained future senator Burton K. Wheeler's first law office. The Lizzie Block was demolished about 1957. At far right is the Owsley Block, which contained the Butte Business College on the upper floor. It was later known as the Medical Arts Building, and burned in 1973.

NORTH MAIN STREET, EARLY 1950S. The famous M&M Bar is prominent on the left in this early-1950s view of the west side of North Main Street. Other 1950s businesses on the left, north from the M&M, are Jim Spier Men's Clothier, Uncles Jeweler, Kruppenheimer Clothes, Klems Shoes, and Green's Cafe. The Hirbour Tower and Hennessy's are on the far right.

MAIN AND BROADWAY STREETS, EARLY 1950S. The First National Bank building, on the left, was completed in 1909 and enlarged in 1915. Just to the left of the Hennessy building, on the northeast corner of Granite and Main Streets, is the Beaver Block, which at one time housed the Silver Bow Bank. The Beaver Block was demolished in 1968, and today, Wells Fargo Bank is located there at 202 North Main Street.

MAIN STREET LOOKING SOUTH ABOUT 1916. The Beaver Block is on the far left of this postcard view looking south across the intersection of Granite and Main Streets. The next large building on the left is Hennessy's. On the far right is the Lewisohn Block. For many years, it housed the M.J. Connell Mercantile Company, which later merged with Hennessy's. The Connell Company installed the first elevator in Butte in this building in 1887.

EAST BROADWAY, PRE-1905. The Hirbour Tower is on the left, and the Butte Hotel is two buildings east of that. City hall, with the clock tower, is prominent on the right, and the buildings on the right edge are the old California Saloon and Brewery (with a triangular peak on the front facade). The California Saloon was one of the oldest saloons in Butte. This structure housing the California Saloon was torn down in 1905.

EAST BROADWAY ABOUT 1915. The new California Saloon and Brewery are the two buildings at right. Among others, Carrie Nation entered this new California Saloon in 1910 for a temperance speech. Later, the second Board of Trade saloon was at this location. The California Saloon location burned in 1969 and is now a parking lot. The Butte Hotel, across from city hall, burned in 1954.

A VIEW IN BUTTE, MONT. SHOWING SCHOOL OF MINES, AND BIG BUTTE.

BIG BUTTE AND WEST BUTTE. Big Butte, Butte's namesake, with an "M" for the Montana School of Mines on painted rhyolite near its peak, is on the right of this 1940 postcard. The Montana School of Mines is at left center, and part of West Butte spreads below it. The students at the Montana School of Mines constructed the "M" in 1910, helping to date photographs of this area.

MCQUEEN AND THE BERKELEY PIT. This postcard from the early- to mid-1960s shows the Berkeley Pit swallowing Meaderville and the Leonard mine. About 13 other major underground mines were also consumed by the Pit. A portion of the community of McQueen is at center. McQueen was mostly gone by 1974, and its Holy Savior School and Church were buried in mine waste rock in 1978. The Continental Pit now occupies the foreground.

CENTERVILLE, EARLY 1960s. Clear Grit Terrace is a small section of Centerville on Butte's north side. The Mountain Con mine and gallows frame is in the background. This postcard displays how close some houses were to the mines and how they were built on terraced hillsides. Centerville was about half Cornish and half Irish.

Seven

SCHOOLS AND CHURCHES

In early Montana, schools and churches were two of the most influential forces in building a community. The first school in what is now Butte was a log cabin on what is now East Broadway Street. It opened in 1866 with private subscriptions from parents. By 1868, the school was a wood-frame building near what became the intersection of Main and Granite Streets. The location of the school moved around from 1868 to 1875. Placer mining declined, and an improvement in schools did not occur until hard-rock mining began to boom in the late 1870s. There was only one teacher through 1875, but then the town and schools began to grow, and 20 teachers were employed by 1886. An organized public school system began, and eventually, 26 public schools and 12 Catholic schools were built in the greater Butte area. Butte High School was established in 1884 and a Catholic high school in 1888. There were also 19 county schools spread throughout what became Silver Bow County. The Butte Business College and the Montana School of Mines were established as well.

At one time there were nine Catholic and eight Methodist churches in Butte. Church membership and attendance declined, and by 2015, there were six Catholic churches and one Methodist church. There were six Baptist churches at one time; one was African American, as was one of the original Methodist churches. There were three Lutheran, two Presbyterian, and one Episcopal church, as well as Serbian churches and Jewish synagogues. A postcard exists showing the B'Nai Israel Reformed Jewish synagogue in Butte (the oldest Jewish congregation in Montana), but the authors do not have a copy. An Orthodox Jewish congregation formed, but did not last long. From about 1920 to the present, a number of other denominations have built churches, a few of which were illustrated with postcards.

Two booklets were helpful for this chapter: Wilma Blewett Puich's *Where We Went to School: 1866–2015* and Robert Mirich's *Butte Churches, Old and New*, both published in 2015.

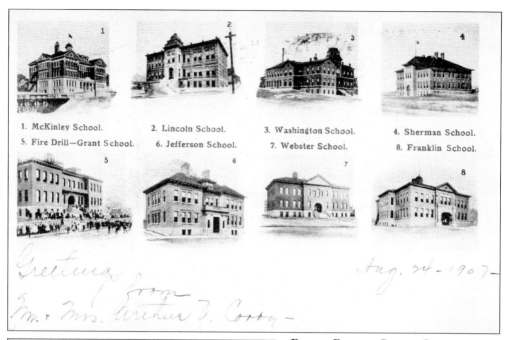

1. McKinley School.   2. Lincoln School.   3. Washington School.   4. Sherman School.
5. Fire Drill—Grant School.   6. Jefferson School.   7. Webster School.   8. Franklin School.

Greeting from Mr. + Mrs. Arthur J. Corby —   *Aug. 24 - 1907 —*

St. Patrick's Parochial School, Butte, Mont.

BUTTE PUBLIC GRADE SCHOOLS, 1907. These eight Butte public schools—McKinley, Lincoln, Washington, Sherman, Grant, Jefferson, Webster, and Franklin—are representative of the many public schools Butte had over its history. The first opened in the winter of 1866, and up until 1875, there was just one teacher and one school. After 1875, as Butte began to grow, 25 additional public grade schools were built.

ST. PATRICK'S PAROCHIAL SCHOOL. St. Patrick's was one of nine Catholic schools in Butte's history. It was built in 1888 at 400 West Park Street and served as both a grade school and a high school until 1908, when the new Butte Central Catholic High School opened at 9 South Idaho Street. St. Patrick's then reverted to a grade school until it was closed in 1969. After much renovation, it became the Mining City Center building.

SECOND BUTTE PUBLIC HIGH SCHOOL. The first Butte Public High School opened in 1884 on East Granite Street and was replaced in 1896 by the high school pictured here on South Idaho Street between Park and Galena Streets. It operated through 1937. After this second high school was vacated by the school district, a fire in 1946 completely destroyed the building.

THIRD BUTTE PUBLIC HIGH SCHOOL. Construction of Butte's third high school began in 1936, and it opened in 1938 at 401 South Wyoming Street with 2,000 students. Its large football stadium was renamed Naranche Stadium in 1943 in honor of Eso Naranche, one of Butte's star athletes, who was killed in combat during World War II. The stadium's field was dirt mixed with cinders until 1982, when grass was planted.

If in these colors you believe,
Put this emblem, on cap or sleeve.

BUTTE HIGH SCHOOL PROMOTIONAL POSTCARD. The citizens of Butte were always zealously supportive of their schools, especially Butte Public High School with its purple and white school colors and its bulldog mascot. During athletic events, cheerleaders, a pep squad, students, and fans would sing out, "We are the Bulldogs, mighty, mighty Bulldogs everywhere we go people want to know who we are, so we tell them."

MONTANA SCHOOL OF MINES. Authorized by the 1893 legislature, the Montana School of Mines' first building (Main Hall) was constructed in 1897 in west Butte, and its doors opened in 1900. Two degrees were offered to the initial 21 students: mining engineering and electrical engineering. From this one building evolved one of the finest engineering schools in the nation, with most students receiving immediate employment upon graduation.

110

1910 SCHOOL OF MINES STUDENT.
Ed (last name unknown) writes
Ransom Cooper Jr. at Syracuse, New
York: "School is going fine. Am
playing left half on the team." He also
was chasing girls and riding Indian
motorcycles. Ransom Cooper Jr. was
from a Great Falls, Montana, family,
and after getting his engineering
degree at Syracuse, he worked for the
ACM at its Great Falls facilities. Of
Ed's fate, nothing is known.

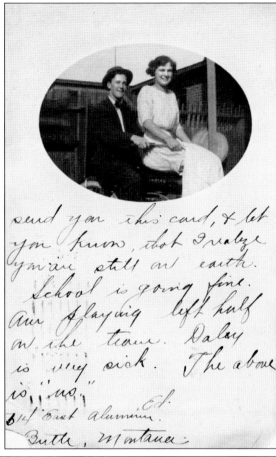

SCHOOL OF MINES, 1930S. As seen
in this postcard, by the 1930s, the
Montana School of Mines, overlooking
the western residential district, had
added a considerable number of new
buildings. It became affiliated with
the University of Montana in 1994
and after several name changes became
Montana Technological University in
2018. Also in 2018, it was named the
number one best value engineering
school in the United States by Best
Value Schools.

603—Montana School of Mines, Butte, Montana

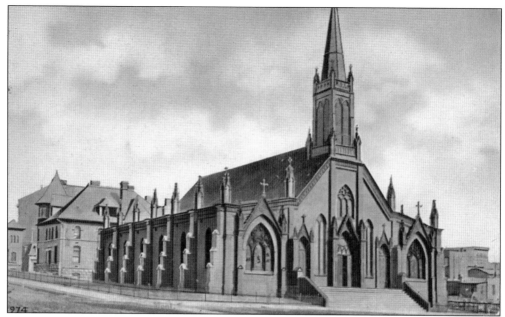

ST. PATRICK'S CATHOLIC CHURCH. St. Patrick's Parish was established around 1879, but construction on the church at the northeast corner of Washington and Mercury Streets did not begin until 1881. The wings on either side of the original main structure were added in 1896. This was the first Catholic church in Butte, and it is sometimes called the "Mother Church of Butte." There were over 4,000 members in 1916.

MOUNTAIN VIEW METHODIST EPISCOPAL CHURCH. This church at the northwest corner of Quartz and Montana Streets was built in 1899. W.A. Clark and W.W. Van Orsdel (Brother Van) laid its cornerstone. It was called the "Mine Owners' Church." One of eight original Methodist churches in Butte, declining membership forced its closure in 2015. It featured superb acoustics and from 2016 to 2018 was the Mountain View Music Hall.

ST. MARY'S CHURCH. This Catholic church was founded in 1902, but its original building on North Wyoming Street burned, and the structure shown on this postcard was built in 1931 at 434 North Main Street. This church and St. Lawrence's Catholic Church at 1306 North Main combined in the 1970s but closed in 1986 due to declining membership, declining availability of priests, and two other Catholic churches within a mile.

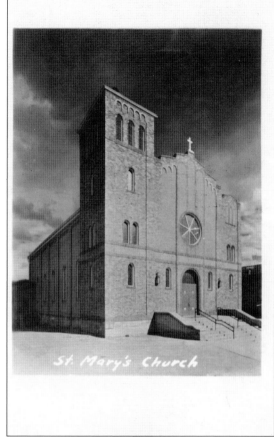

SACRED HEART CATHOLIC CHURCH. This church and rectory at 448 East Park Street was completed in late 1903. It burned in November 1912, but the first floor survived and was used as a parochial school until 1969. A replacement church building in the Spanish Mission style was built nearby at 363 East Park Street in 1913 and served through 1970. Both buildings were demolished in 1974.

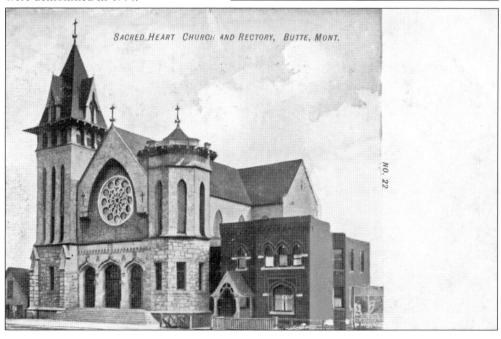

CHRISTIAN SCIENCE CHURCH
BUTTE, MONT.

222—Immaculate Conception Church, Butte, Mont.

CHRISTIAN SCIENCE CHURCH. The Christian Science church was organized in Butte in 1893, but the neoclassical building seen in this postcard at 229 North Montana Street was not built until 1920. Membership dwindled over the years, and in 2014, private investors bought the historic building at auction for $52,500 and rented it to Harvest Church through 2019.

IMMACULATE CONCEPTION CATHOLIC CHURCH. This church at 410 North Western Avenue is featured in a number of more recent postcards of Butte. Its iconic tower serves as a navigation landmark. The parish was formed in 1906, and many additions occurred to the original building. The church seen on this postcard was completed in 1941. In the 1950s, its elementary school had almost 500 students.

ASSEMBLY OF GOD CHURCH. The Butte Assembly of God Church at 2055 Florence Avenue, with its unusual architecture, is a relatively recent addition to Butte's churches. The first pastor was Rev. Leo Hinton, who served from 1939 to 1947. The congregation was active in 2020 in the same building.

ST. ANN'S CHURCH AND SCHOOL. St. Ann's Parish began in 1917. Its school at 2400 Kossuth Street is featured on this postcard in 1949. Like other Catholic schools, it closed in 1969 and now serves as offices for the parish. The new, modern round church and tower of St. Ann's at nearby 2100 Farragut Avenue on the "Flats" was started in 1965, and its architecture was initially somewhat controversial.

THE COVENANT MISSION CHURCH. The church in this 1950s real-photo postcard, with its unusual architecture, apparently was originally occupied by a breakaway branch of a Swedish Lutheran church. Located at 1027 South Main Street, the building has recently been occupied by the Grace and Truth Pentecostal Church, affiliated with the United Pentecostal Church.

RALLY DAY AND CRADLE ROLL. This common form of postcard was used mostly by non-Catholic churches to encourage parents to bring their new children to church. The baby, Leroy Glenn Seymour, grew up in Butte, graduated in business administration from the University of Montana in 1938, married in 1941, and enlisted in the military in 1942. He died in 1971 at Cascade, Montana, without children of his own.

Eight

SURROUNDING AREAS AND MISCELLANEOUS VIEWS

Silver Bow County was established on February 16, 1881, from the southern portion of the original Deer Lodge County. Although Butte was always the biggest town, over time, Silver Bow County had 20 towns with post offices. Ten of these towns lost their post office or became ghost towns prior to the postcard boom starting in 1905. These lost towns include Anderson, Burlington, Feely, Gunderson (a previous name for Meaderville), Moose Creek, Mount Horeb, Norwood, Onge, Red Mountain City, and South Butte. Ten towns had post offices during the early and prime postcard production periods: Butte, Divide, Grace, Gregson, Meaderville (formerly Gunderson), Melrose, Ramsay, Rocker, Silver Bow, and Walkerville. The post office at South Butte was gone prior to the postcard period, but it survived as a substation, and there are postcards with a "So. Butte Substation" postmark.

All the towns mentioned above can be considered part of the Butte–Silver Bow consolidated community. Also part of the Butte community were named places without post offices, such as Williamsburg, a German settlement in southwest Butte with two breweries, and Nissler, near Silver Bow junction. Within and immediately surrounding Butte, there were named communities such as Centerville, Corktown, Dublin Gulch, Cabbage Patch, Muckerville, Butchertown, Stringtown, Seldom Seen, East Side, McQueen, Finn Town, and others. Some of these towns and areas are mentioned in previous chapters, but additional postcards and information are provided here. All of Silver Bow County, from Gregson in the northwest to Melrose in the far south and Grace in the southeast, was part of the mercantile, social, and recreational character of Butte.

Other interesting types of postcards related to Butte and the surrounding area are also illustrated. These include leather and wooden postcards, which were legal to mail at one time. Postcards of adjacent water sources for Butte, a recreational area, and two postcards of *Our Lady of the Rockies*, an important newer landmark of the greater Butte community, are also included.

Gregson Hot Springs Hotel, Natatorium 200x64, Boyce-Butte, 17 Miles from Butte, Mont.

GREGSON HOT SPRINGS. George and Eli Gregson purchased the hot springs and surrounding acreage in 1869, and there have been many owners since. This postcard shows the Gregson Hot Springs buildings in 1913, shortly before they burned in December 1914. In August 1912, a year before this postcard was mailed, the Butte Miner's Union held a picnic at Gregson Hot Springs, and a fight broke out with the Anaconda Smeltermen. Two men were killed and many injured.

GREGSON HOT SPRINGS, 1917. George Forsythe bought Gregson Hot Springs in 1916 and constructed new and expanded buildings to attract tourists in addition to locals. This real-photo postcard shows an early view of the new Gregson Hot Springs. By 1971, the resort had deteriorated to such an extent that it closed. New construction began in 1972, and the Silver Bow County resort is now known as Fairmont Hot Springs Resort.

Melrose, Montana, Looking North.

Does this look at all familiar to you? The view was taken in July 1909, from the top of a freight car. E. Hw.

MELROSE, MONTANA, LOOKING NORTH. Melrose, at the very southern tip of Silver Bow County, was established in 1881 as a construction point on the Utah & Northern Railroad. It continued as a town serving the freighting needs of the Hecla mines to the west and ranching. This 1909 postcard, looking north toward Butte, shows the railroad tracks, depot, businesses along Hecla Street to the left, and residences to the right.

98   Melrose, Montana.

BUSINESS SECTION, MELROSE, 1910. At far right in this postcard view is the brick Iowa House, a railroad hotel still standing today, though not as a hotel. Next door is a saloon. The one-story brick commercial building at right center also still stands. Today, Melrose mainly serves as a small ranching community and an angler's stop on the Big Hole River.

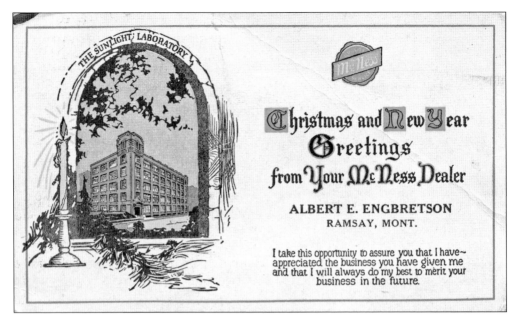

RAMSAY, MONTANA. Ramsay was established in 1916 as a company town for DuPont, which built a munitions plant there during World War I. This Christmas and New Year's greetings postcard was sent from Ramsay in 1928 by Albert Engbretson, a door-to-door salesman for McNess products. Similar to its business competitor Watkins, McNess sold flavorings, extracts, seasonings, salves, ointments, and home remedies. Both are still in business today.

HENRY'S DRIVE INN. Henry's Drive Inn, owned and operated by Ronald and Florence Young, was six miles west of Butte at Nissler on US Highway 10 near its junction with US Highway 91. At the time, radio station KXLF was directly opposite. Henry's rated its coffee as the "Best in the West." This postcard was photographed and published by the prolific Cecil Nixon.

THE LEAKY ROOF. This real-photo postcard of a Rocky Mountain "rack jabbit" advertises another business at Nissler Junction: the Leaky Roof tavern, owned and operated by Carl Gillespie. An advertisement on a 1951 map of the Butte area indicated that Gillespie had owned the establishment since 1939. It stated: "All work and no play makes Jack a dull boy." In addition to drinks, the tavern also served sandwiches and short orders.

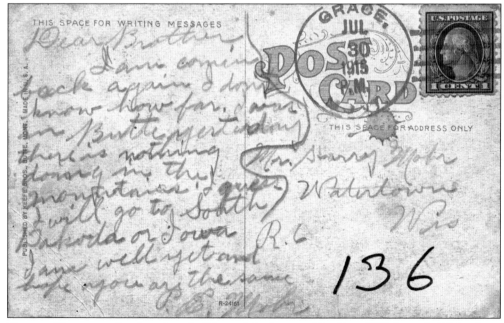

GRACE, MONTANA. Few have heard of Grace. It had a post office from 1882 through 1926 and was in far southeast Silver Bow County. In the 1880s, it was near the short-lived mining towns of Mount Horeb and Red Mountain City. By the time this postcard was sent from Grace in 1915, it was a stop on the Chicago, Milwaukee & St. Paul Railroad. In the 1920 census, there were 79 inhabitants.

THE BIG HOLE DAM AND POWER HOUSE, WHERE BUTTE GETS ITS WATER.

BUTTE'S WATER SUPPLY. The Butte Water Company was established in 1898, and by 1899, a dam and pumping station were constructed on the Big Hole River near Divide, Montana, to supply water to Butte. With improvements over the years (1906, 1916, 1930, 1954), over 15 million gallons of water a day could be moved 27 miles over the Continental Divide to Butte. This postcard is from about 1916, when three water pumps were in operation.

POWER FOR THE WATER COMPANY. This government postal card was sent from Divide in 1905 by pumping station engineer C.J. Wood to company headquarters in Butte. The reverse acknowledges receipt of a carload (90,000 pounds) of slack (fine coal and coal dust) to power the pumps. Two years later, the power for the pumps was supplied by electricity, and coal was no longer used.

Clearmont on the Lakes, Butte, Mont.

LAKE AVOCA. Clearmont on the Lakes was a resort on man-made Lake Avoca, created in 1894. The lake was used recreationally during summer and winter by the citizens of Butte, and ice was harvested there in winter by the Butte Ice Company. In 1938, the property was sold to the Butte Country Club, which had the lake drained. The location is now the Butte Country Club Golf Course.

THE PARK AT THE BASIN CREEK RESERVOIR, WITH THE DAM IN THE DISTANCE. BUTTE, MONT. 67483

BASIN CREEK RESERVOIR AND PARK. The lower dam of the Basin Creek Reservoir was originally completed in 1895 and then raised to 131 feet in 1913. Complementary to the reservoir was a park and pavilion below the dam established for the enjoyment of Butte's citizens. The reservoir provides some of Butte's fresh water, and in 1917, the *Butte Miner* newspaper claimed that "Nowhere is the Quality of Butte's Crystal Water Excelled."

OUR LADY OF THE ROCKIES. The 90-foot-tall *Our Lady of the Rockies* was conceived in 1979 by Bob O'Bill of Butte when his wife recovered from cancer. The statue, on private land on the "East Ridge," was originally to be only about five feet tall. His idea grew into a volunteer effort to design and erect this much larger statue. (Photograph by Steven Hadnagy.)

THE LADY OVERLOOKS BUTTE. One of the largest statues in the United States was completed on December 20, 1985, after six years of work. She is dedicated to "all women, especially mothers," and from the top of the Continental Divide, she watches over Butte. The only access to the site is through summer and early fall tours conducted by the private Our Lady of the Rockies Foundation. (Photograph by Joe Vukovich.)

MERRY CHRISTMAS AND HAPPY NEW YEAR. In the late 1910s, the Boughton-Robbins Company of Spokane, Washington, produced a series of hand-colored Christmas holiday postcards featuring scenes from all over Montana. It takes many years of collecting to complete the set. This scene of the "Richest Hill in the World" surrounded by green trees and a lake is the Butte card.

BUTTE FELT PENNANT GREETING POSTCARD. A popular type of greeting card to send to the folks back home was the pennant postcard. This postcard asking if she is still remembered was sent in 1918 by a daughter in Butte to her mother in Roanoke, Missouri. These and other postcards were the equivalent to today's short emails or text messages.

W.J. Rundle Family Photograph.
The real-photo postcard was commonly used to send family photographs to relatives and friends. Sent from Butte on November 10, 1914, to a friend in Granite, Montana, the message on this card reads, "I started work the day after I got here and have worked steady ever since. There are thousands of men out of work here (as a result of union unrest earlier in 1914). The photo is myself, Eliza, and children."

Butte's Strong Democratic Party. Butte has long been, and is still today, a stronghold of the Democratic party. This November 1, 1912, postcard urges a straight-ticket vote for Democratic legislative candidates. The card was sent to A.W. Noble, the proprietor of Noble Drugs, whose advertising postcard appears in chapter four. In a rare deviation from Democrats, Socialist Lewis J. Duncan served as mayor from 1911 to 1914.

CONSIDER THIS !

The Democratic legislative ticket is composed of representative business and labor men.

2 Labor Union Men.	1 Banker.
1 Salesman.	1 Surveyor.
1 Lawyer.	1 Contractor.

The Democratic legislative ticket is a clean ticket and represents clean progressive government.

The Democratic legislative ticket will further your interests in whatever walk of life you follow.

Past Democratic legislatures have emblazoned upon the statutes of Montana every creditable humanitarian law.

The Democratic legislative ticket is a winning ticket. Why sacrifice your vote in visionary "party" balloting.

VOTE IT STRAIGHT !

NOVELTY LEATHER POSTCARD FROM BUTTE. From about 1905 to 1909, novelty leather postcards were a fad in the United States. Some ladies collected them and sewed them together to make pillow coverings. The US Postal Service banned them in 1909 because of the problems they caused with sorting machines and their failure to hold stamps well. This card, postmarked in Butte on October 28, 1909, was late in the legal period of use.

NOVELTY WOODEN POSTCARD FROM BUTTE. Another popular novelty postcard in the early 1900s was the wooden postcard, with art and a message burned into the card with woodburning tools. This card was mailed in 1907 from Butte to 223 South Jackson Street in Butte with the message "I'll be busy all next week in Butte."

Discover Thousands of Local History Books
Featuring Millions of Vintage Images

Arcadia Publishing, the leading local history publisher in the United States, is committed to making history accessible and meaningful through publishing books that celebrate and preserve the heritage of America's people and places.

Find more books like this at
www.arcadiapublishing.com

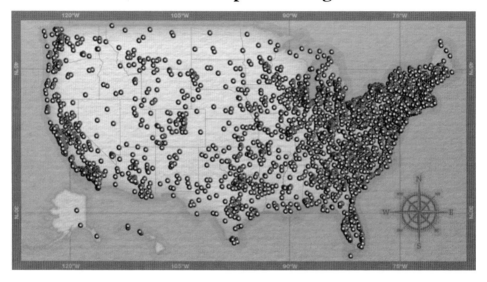

Search for your hometown history, your old stomping grounds, and even your favorite sports team.

Consistent with our mission to preserve history on a local level, this book was printed in South Carolina on American-made paper and manufactured entirely in the United States. Products carrying the accredited Forest Stewardship Council (FSC) label are printed on 100 percent FSC-certified paper.

MADE IN THE USA